WHEN A CATHOLIC MARRIES A NON-CATHOLIC

WHEN A
CATHOLIC
MARRIES
A
NON-CATHOLIC

ROBERT J. HATER

ST. ANTHONY MESSENGER PRESS

Cincinnati, Ohio

RESCRIPT

In accord with the *Code of Canon Law*, I hereby grant my permission to publish *When A Catholic Marries a Non-Catholic*, written by Robert J. Hater.

Most Reverend Carl K. Moeddel
Vicar General and Auxiliary Bishop
Archdiocese of Cincinnati
Cincinnati, Ohio
August 8, 2006

The permission to publish is a declaration that a book or pamphlet is considered to be free from doctrinal or moral error. It is not implied that those who have granted the permission to publish agree with the contents, opinions or statements expressed.

Scripture passages have been taken from *New Revised Standard Version Bible*, copyright ©1989 by the Division of Christian Education of the National Council of the Churches of Christ in the U.S.A., and used by permission.
All rights reserved.

Cover and book design by Mark Sullivan
Cover image ©istockphoto.com/Kevin Pipher

LIBRARY OF CONGRESS CATALOGING-IN-PUBLICATION DATA
Hater, Robert J.
When a Catholic marries a non-Catholic / Robert J. Hater.
p. cm.
Includes bibliographical references and index.
ISBN-13: 978-0-86716-678-1 (pbk. : alk. paper)
ISBN-10: 0-86716-678-9 (pbk. : alk. paper)
1. Interfaith marriage. 2. Marriage—Religious aspects—Catholic Church. I. Title.

HQ1031.H32 2006
261.8'35843—dc22

2006022327

ISBN-13 978-0-86716-678-1
ISBN-10 0-86716-678-9

Copyright ©2006, Robert J. Hater

Published by St. Anthony Messenger Press
28 W. Liberty St.
Cincinnati, OH 45202
www.AmericanCatholic.org

Printed in the United States of America.

Printed on acid-free paper.

06 07 08 09 10 5 4 3 2 1

This book is dedicated to my deceased parents,
Stanley C. and Olivia L. Hater.
They created a Catholic home environment that grounded our
family members in faith, hope, love and gratitude.

I also dedicate the book to my sisters,
Joan Marie Kohl and Mary Ann Haubner
and my brother, Thomas S. Hater.

[A C K N O W L E D G M E N T S]

In writing this book, I am indebted to many people, especially those interfaith married couples who encouraged me to write it and later critiqued it. I am also grateful to all those who evaluated the text. In particular, the following played a special role in its composition: Rev. Harry J. Meyer, Rev. Joseph R. Binzer, Rev. Alan Hirt, O.F.M., Rev. Thomas A. Snodgrass, Peg Davis, Dr. Bud Newsom, James and Jennifer Hudgens, Msgr. Fred Easton, Sr. Victoria Vondenberger, R.S.M., J.C.L., Rita Balcom, Jan Utrecht, Lisa Biedenbach and Kathleen Carroll. I am especially grateful to Peg Davis, the former Director of Family Life for the Archdiocese of Cincinnati, for her invaluable comments and for honoring me in writing the Preface of the book. I also thank the Ecumenical Committee of St. Susanna Parish, Mason, Ohio, for their suggestions.

[C O N T E N T S]

When a Catholic Marries a Non-Catholic is a timely new book for the national, diocesan, parish and personal levels. It is written for those personally involved in mixed marriages and those who minister to them. As it goes to press, the U.S. Conference of Catholic Bishops (USCCB) continues their research to begin writing a pastoral on the sacrament of marriage. Many dioceses, including my own, are further developing premarital guidelines in light of recent societal developments. Parishes are seeking ways to respond more pastorally to the needs of parishioners in interfaith marriages. Couples preparing for marriage and those already in mixed marriages are seeking support. This book is written in response.

When my parents married some fifty-plus years ago, it was almost unheard of for folks to go outside their religious sphere to choose a spouse. It was not difficult to find a suitable mate right within the neighborhood, and since the church was the center of the community, the mate was usually of like faith. But the later half of the twentieth century exploded in communication systems and mobility. Along with it came the blending of cultures and family diversity, including an acceptance of religious diversity within the marital relationship.

Currently over 40 percent of those couples coming to the Catholic church to participate in the sacrament of marriage are of "mixed" religions. At one time, many priests would have encouraged the non-Catholic to enroll in convert instruction and become Catholic before the "I do's." Now the Catholic church recognizes the value and grace of other faiths, and marriage ministers are challenged to extend not only a hospitable welcome but also support for these couples.

When a Catholic Marries a Non-Catholic is timely in addressing the challenges and blessings such couples present to the church and those in marriage ministry. This book offers a positive perspective toward lifelong marital unions of mixed marriages. The reader, whether a member of the clergy, a lay minister or a spouse, will find suggestions for sustenance, growth and nurturing. Intriguing questions for reflection are posed at the end of each chapter helping us to explore our own biases and need for further growth, and deepening our understanding.

Father Hater candidly remarks that spouses of equal faith practicing the same religion seem more evenly yoked and have a smoother road for preparation and marriage. But he is quick to point out that couples of mixed marriage can also serve as models of the graces that marriage can offer to married couples and to the community as well.

While holding clearly to the tenets of the Catholic faith and the view of Christ among us all, Father Hater speaks with a tone of compassion, respect, wisdom and gentleness. It is my firm conviction as a family minister that when all couples and families experience such a welcoming environment, then a vibrant community of faith grows stronger.

Margaret Callender Davis
Former Director of Family Life Office
Archdiocese of Cincinnati

Marriage

is changing in the United States. Cultural and religious norms that once kept family life in a close-knit structure of parents and children no longer exist. Social pressures affect the fiber of marriage itself. Once, Catholics and members of other religions discouraged their children from dating and marrying someone belonging to another faith. While still true in some cases, this has largely disappeared. About 40 percent of all Catholic weddings in the Archdiocese of Cincinnati in the last several years were mixed marriages.[1]

The number of mixed marriages in all religious denominations throughout the United States is increasing. We must look more deeply into the challenges and blessings associated with interfaith unions and make new, positive efforts to support these couples in their love for God, each other and their families. A positive approach welcomes couples entering mixed marriages into our parishes and makes them feel at home.[2] Regarding mixed marriages with hope does not minimize the challenges that they present, but recognizes the blessings that they can afford to spouses, children and the faith community.

The Second Vatican Council says, "The intimate partnership of life and the love which constitutes the married state has been established by the creator and endowed by him with its own proper laws.... For God himself is the author of marriage...".[3] These words apply to all marriages. By their very nature, marriages are blessings from God. The Council invites us to see all marriages as reflections of God's love.

Interfaith couples (see page 10 for an explanation of the various terms used throughout this book) need support from their families and churches. A focus on the spirituality of marriage is an excellent way to begin with couples who come for marriage preparation. Even if a couple has a strong faith commitment and regularly attends church, this can be a time to deepen their understanding of faith and the sacraments. If a couple has weak faith (or no faith), this is the time for pastoral outreach, evangelization and formation.

Marriage is a life-altering decision. Those who have made the choice to marry have already embraced a significant change; many of them are open to examining the role of faith in their lives. Often, couples don't know where to get married or where to turn for spiritual advice. Some do not belong to a church and need help from parents or friends to find a church in which to get married and someone to perform the ceremony.

Rather than contrasting mixed marriages with the marriage of two Catholics, celebrating them as lifelong marital unions blessed by God provides a positive perspective. Such an outlook on all marriages contrasts with the tenets of our throwaway society. The prevalent philosophy, "If this partner doesn't work out, I can get another," can lead to trial marriages, people cohabiting outside of marriage and adulterous affairs. We have all seen the human and societal toll taken by this shortsighted view. The Catholic approach to marriage offers an alternative: seeing marriage as the intimate union of a man and a woman, involving ever-deepening and evolving love, reflecting God's love, lasting a lifetime.

When a Catholic Marries a Non-Catholic invites couples entering mixed marriages to do so with hope. It encourages them to consider seriously the challenges of their union, examine their faith and decide whether they are ready to marry. It asks them to take their faith seriously, to see the implications of a mixed marriage and to commit themselves to a religiously based family.

This book also asks interfaith couples to see their marriages through the eyes of faith. It asks them to reflect on their blessings and, especially, to respect one another's faith. In so doing, they can better realize that faith is a wonderful gift that they give each other and their children. Living their faith celebrates their joys, strengthens them and affords them the happiness that Jesus promised to those who love him.

A New Look

A POSITIVE START

Their

elderly father was Christian, a lifelong member of the United Church of Christ and a leader and active member in that congregation for decades. Their mother was a lifelong Catholic, also active in her parish for decades and devout in her practice of the faith. Their five children were educated in Catholic schools, and most were practicing Catholics as adults. When the father died after a lengthy illness and the funeral plans began to take shape, the couple's adult children faced the issue of how to celebrate their father's life and his faith tradition yet recognize the needs of the survivors for something "a little bit Catholic" that would not insult or demean in any way the United Church of Christ members.

The children soon learned that the pastor of the United Church of Christ was very much attuned to the family's needs and he suggested including the pastor of their mother's church as a co-celebrant at the funeral service. The two pastors knew each other, fortunately, and were able to plan a funeral service that spoke authentically to two faith traditions. Each pastor had the opportunity to proclaim Scripture, to preach and to bless the coffin. Hymns were chosen from both church hymnals, and members of both churches attended the funeral service. The United Church of Christ pastor in his homily recognized the mutual respect that husband and wife had had for each other's faith for the fifty-five years of their mixed marriage and how each spouse willingly supported the other's church activities. In fact, the pastor said, the couple was so active in each other's church that each church thought both spouses were members of their congregations! The pastor said that the couple, Homer and Angela, had a wonderful ecumenical marriage before it was "cool" to be ecumenical. After the moving funeral service, the children heard many comments that it had been a real tribute to the couple's mixed marriage and that it was an inspiring celebration of death as well as marriage.

In reflecting on stories like this one, Dr. Mark, a retired marriage counselor, said, "Not minimizing the challenges associated with mixed marriages, one thing stands out when I reflect on the sincere couples that came to me for help. As I listened to them, I became more and more convinced of how different religious beliefs bring special blessings to a marriage. This was the case with Homer and Angela. If only, couples would maximize the strengths coming from their different faith traditions! Each marriage can be a gift and blessing from God, like Homer's and Angela's was."

Each religious faith has its own beliefs, rituals and history that affect the marriages of their members. These include the basic beliefs and traditions that frame the attitudes, preparations, celebrations and married life of its members. Even within the same faith tradition, the faith reaches different expressions in various cultures. Roman Catholics celebrate marriages differently today than before Vatican II. Byzantine Catholics and other ethnic Catholics include elements of their traditional cultures in their marriage celebrations. Some religious traditions allow greater flexibility than others do when their members marry those of other faith traditions.

Such differences lead to different requirements for the marriage of members of one religious tradition and those of another faith. Roman Catholics and Orthodox Jews, for example, are bound by stricter norms than their counterparts in many Protestant churches. For this reason, it is important to clarify from the outset the norms and procedures that are incumbent upon couples who marry someone who is not of their faith.

LANGUAGE FOR MIXED MARRIAGES

Suzie approached me about celebrating her wedding to Bill. I knew her as an energetic and faithful Catholic teenager before she left for college. Then I lost track of her. When she called, Suzie said, "Father Bob, I was away at college for four years. After I graduated, I lived in Denver for five more years. There, I met Bill. He's a great guy, but not Catholic. Will you marry us?"

The way Suzie asked me to officiate at their marriage is similar to the way that many engaged couples contact a parish or a priest. They want to get married, convinced that the other person is the "right one," but they know little about church policies and procedures. Suzie knew that she had to indicate at the outset that Bill was Protestant. She did not realize, however, that marrying him would be different than marrying the man she previously dated, who was Jewish. She didn't know the right language to use.

The question of the right language is not easy to decide when dealing with marriages between a Catholic and a person who is not Catholic. In researching materials for this book, it became clear that all Catholic diocesan marriage guidelines do not use the same terms. One diocesan guideline may refer to the marriage of a Catholic and a non-Catholic Christian as an *ecumenical marriage*, while another may call it an *interchurch marriage*. Dioceses may refer to such marriages as "mixed religion" on the marriage forms. One diocese may use the term *interreligious marriage* for the marriage of a Catholic and a non-baptized person, though another may call it an *interfaith marriage.* To complicate matters more, the term *interfaith marriage* often is used in some guidelines or publications to refer to the marriage of a Catholic to anyone who is not Catholic. The current situation leads to confusion.

To simplify the terminology used in this book, it begins by indicating key sections in the 1983 *Code of Canon Law* pertaining to mixed marriages.[4] Here, *mixed marriage* means the marriage between a Catholic and a person who is not Catholic. If a mixed marriage is between a Catholic and a validly baptized Christian, *permission* must be granted to enter such a union. This can be given by the diocesan bishop, vicar general, episcopal vicar or anyone delegated by the diocesan bishop for this purpose. If a mixed marriage is between a Catholic and an unbaptized person, a *dispensation* from disparity of cult is required (Canons 1086 and 1129). A central point in the *Code's* approach to the marriage of a Catholic and a non-Catholic is whether or not the non-Catholic is validly baptized.

This book keeps these points in mind in the use of terminology for the marriage of a Catholic and a non-Catholic. *Mixed marriage* is used here as the umbrella or general term which refers to the marriage between a Catholic and a person who is not Catholic. When a mixed marriage is between a Catholic and a validly baptized Christian, the expression *mixed marriage between a Catholic and a baptized Christian* is used. Examples are the marriage of a Catholic and a Lutheran, Episcopalian or Methodist. When a mixed marriage is between a Catholic and an unbaptized person, the expression *mixed marriage between a Catholic and an unbaptized person* is used. Examples are the marriage of a Catholic and a Jew, Muslim, Buddhist, atheist or agnostic.[5]

The marriage between a baptized man and a baptized

woman who have been baptized Catholic or in any valid Christian baptism is a sacrament, provided they are free of any impediment. The concept of sacramentality is central to the church's different classifications of marriage. Two baptized Catholics profess their Christian faith as full members of the Catholic church. Hence, when they marry, they enter into a sacramental relationship of love, rooted in their baptism. They seal this love with their reception of the Eucharist and later in their marital union as man and wife.

As mentioned previously, the *Code*'s classification of marriages between Catholics and persons who are not Catholic centers on whether or not the non-Catholic spouse has been validly baptized.

When a Catholic marries a person validly baptized in another Christian community, their marriage is rooted in the Christian faith through their baptism. This union is sacramental, but lacks, however, full incorporation into the Catholic community, since one partner is not Catholic. Permission is required to enter such a union.

When a Catholic marries a person who is not baptized, no sacramental union exists. Since one person does not profess the Christian faith, the church exercises more caution in granting a dispensation for such marriages. Though they do not participate in the grace of the sacrament of marriage, both partners benefit from God's love and help (grace) through their good lives and beliefs.

The church does not allow mixed marriages without permission or a dispensation. The church makes clear to such couples that their marriages will be more challenging from the perspective of faith, and greater dangers exist for the faith of the Catholic person. Special challenges exist as well when it comes to raising future children in the Catholic faith. For these reasons, the church requires the Catholic party to make special promises regarding the faith of the Catholic party and the baptism and education of the children. It is hoped that, in making these promises, the Catholic person has properly considered the potential difficulties and is confident that they can be overcome.

There are various kinds of mixed marriages. In particular, the following kinds are noteworthy:

Marriages Between Catholics and Eastern Orthodox Christians
Marriages between Catholics and Eastern Orthodox Christians fall under special canonical and pastoral norms. Both churches share a consistent belief on many doctrinal issues. Both churches have valid orders, since the line of apostolic succession has not been broken.[6] Both acknowledge the same sacraments, priesthood and Eucharist. Solid marriage preparation helps the marital unity between a Roman Catholic and an Eastern Orthodox spouse. As the *Directory of the Application of Principles and Norms of Ecumenism* says, "Diversity in liturgical life and private devotion can be made to encourage rather than hinder family prayer."[7]

Marriages Between Catholics and Protestants
Church laws and regulations for Catholics marrying Episcopalians and all Protestants are the same. Even though Episcopalian and Lutheran churches are closer to the Roman Catholic Church in beliefs, practices and ecclesial orientation than other Christian churches, the members of all Christian churches come under the same norms when Catholics marry members of these denominations. Church laws applying to such unions include the same canonical and pastoral norms for place, ministers, dispensations/permissions, reception of communion, celebrating a wedding Mass and the presider at the ceremony.

Marriages Between Catholics and Jews

Even though Catholics and Jews share a common religious heritage, marriages between them offer special challenges. In particular, "The Catholic community needs to be aware that the marriage of a Jew to one who is not, as well as a rabbi's presence at such a ceremony, is problematic for the Jewish community. Judaism is not only a matter of one's personal religious choice but of belonging to a people with ties to the land and state of Israel as well as traditions and values that permeate the home in religious and social celebrations."[8] Even though a dispensation can be obtained to celebrate a Catholic/Jewish wedding at a neutral place with a civil magistrate or rabbi, real challenges exist when it comes to the family life of a committed Jew and a committed Catholic.

Marriages Between Catholics and Muslims, Buddhists and Hindus

With the growing influx of ethnic populations into the United States from Asia, the Near East and Africa, our parishes increasingly face challenges when dealing with marriages between Catholics and Muslims, Buddhists, Hindus and members of other religious traditions. Great sensitivity must be shown to these traditions without minimizing the challenges that differences in culture and religious beliefs bring. Acknowledging such religious and cultural differences, "It is a dialogue which can become the basis of a human relationship of mutual trust, inner peace, and mutual esteem that contributes to the bond of marriage according to the will of the Creator."[9]

Marriages Between Catholics and Agnostics or Atheists

Even though marriages of Catholics to agnostics or atheists present special problems, the Catholic party has the opportunity in such marriages to give testimony to belief in the Lord Jesus, his

Mixed Marriage:
Marriage between a Catholic and a person who is not Catholic.

Mixed Religion Marriage:
Marriage between a Catholic and another baptized Christian (but not Catholic) person.

Interfaith Couple:
A Catholic and a person who is not Catholic planning or involved in a mixed marriage.

Interfaith Family:
A family resulting from a mixed marriage.[10]

Eastern Rite Catholics, whose Churches are in union with Rome, follow the same general norms as Latin Rite Catholics, when they are married to Latin Rite Catholics in Latin Rite Catholic parishes.[11] However, when one spouse is an Eastern Rite Catholic, they must be married by a priest (not a deacon) for validity.

message and the beliefs and practices of the Catholic church. In this regard, "It is most important both that the non-believing spouse acknowledge the freedom of the Catholic spouse to worship and baptize and raise the children as Catholics, and that the Catholic partner has a due respect for the dignity of the atheist spouse's conscience and personal choice."[12]

Many atheists and agnostics are outstanding, moral persons with solid values. The fact that they do not explicitly believe in God, or are not sure that God exists, doesn't make them bad. Often, they are authentically honest and socially conscious. Some have not thought through the issue of God, others have had a traumatic experience that turned them away from God, still others are not sure about God or have consciously decided not to believe.

Atheists and agnostics are God's children. Many of their marriages are loving and fruitful unions that last until death. In dealing with a Catholic marrying an atheist or agnostic, it is better to look at who the person is, rather than what he or she professes. This approach does not minimize the challenges of such marriages. It reminds us that God can bless all marriages. Sometimes, a Christian spouse can set that kind of example, offer that degree of love, and profess that type of faith that leads a nonbelieving spouse to God.

The norms regulating various types of marriage vary according to the situation. They are too complex to address here, but clarity about the type of mixed marriage that one enters is important.[13] In each case, it is wise for a couple to inquire about their situation from a priest or marriage minister.

ALL MARRIAGES: GIFTED BY GOD

"Christian interfaith families are a gift both for our churches and for the whole Church of Jesus Christ. The creativity and longing for a unity that can be visibly manifest, often expressed by members of such families, can serve as a witness to the whole Church."[14] These words are found in the introduction of *Interfaith Families: Resources for Ecumenical Hope*, a book for families of a mixed marriage. They suggest the positive tone necessary to support and assist interfaith couples. All marriages begin with God's love. This love penetrates the hearts and souls of men and women who love one another. Their attraction for each other goes far deeper than their religious affiliation. It is rooted in the core of who they are. Their fundamental identity as persons is rooted in God's creative activity. God's love is so great that the divine creator chose to share it with them. This love is the greatest gift God can offer, for God is love.

God is love and shares this love with every married couple. *Interfaith Families* gives a beautiful reflection on God's creative designs when it says:

> The idea of marriage as a covenant is based on scripture,
> in which the Lord enters into covenant with God's people

and calls them into covenant with God and with one another. The first such covenant is the covenant with creation in which God created human beings male and female. God gives us to one another for mutual help and comfort, to live in fidelity to one another "in plenty and in want, in joy and in sorrow, in sickness and in health, through all their days."[15]

God could have created in many different ways, but from the beginning, as Genesis tells us, God shares divine love through the love of men and women. Because this love is so penetrating and definitive, human love is a foretaste of God's love. No fuller expression of divine love exists on earth than spousal love. God imbedded into men and women the attractive force of this love to continue the divine creative activity. All creation leads up to this love and reflects it. The built-in attraction of the rest of nature, which attracts the male and female members of each species to one another, is brought to perfection in the human race in the conscious and voluntary selection of a spouse. God gave us marriage for the "well-being of the whole human family, the proper ordering of family life, and the birth and nurture of children."[16]

Reflecting on the blessings that God bestows on all marriages, we need also to remember the challenges that mixed marriages, especially disparity-of-worship marriages, present. Such challenges are recognized by various religious denominations. Some religions, like that of Orthodox Jews and the Amish, actively discourage or prohibit mixed marriages.[17] Even those which allow such marriages do so reluctantly.

Though I was well acquainted with the Catholic church's view on mixed marriages, I was surprised to find that we were not in the minority in holding this view. Shortly after my ordination, I participated in a seminar on mixed marriages. It was held at a public university and was geared to college-age students. In her opening address, a Protestant minister indicated that her church strongly discouraged mixed marriages. Calling on extensive pastoral experience, she described the problems associated with them and how such marriages often fail. When it was my turn to speak, I agreed with her. Up to that time, I had not realized that many Protestant churches, like the Catholic church, recognized the challenges that exist in mixed marriages.

Today, even though many denominations are open to mixed marriages, the challenges to make them healthy and happy still exist. I experienced a success story when I met Benjamin and Sue, and their family. Each Sunday at the 10:15 Mass, they would sit in the front of church. Ben never went to Communion—the only indication I had that he might not be Catholic. When I responded to their invitation to dinner, I learned that Ben was Jewish. Their household featured numerous signs of the Catholic and Jewish faiths. Their mealtime prayer reflected both traditions. I spent a wonderful evening of fun, food and good cheer with them. They welcomed me in a way that I rarely experience. Their children, ages three to nine, are well-adjusted, practicing Catholics, enriched by the faith of both parents.

As I got to know Ben and Sue, they told me of the difficulties they experienced by having two faith traditions in their marriage. Their words reflected mutual love and respect, as they discussed the struggles to sort out their personal convictions and their children's religious formation. On the surface, Sue seemed more religious than Ben, but I soon realized that his belief in reform Judaism was equally solid.

They discussed the promises Sue made when they prepared for their marriage. In these promises, she reaffirmed her faith in Jesus, agreed to continue the practice her faith in the Catholic church, do her best to share this faith with their children, and have them baptized and raised as Catholics. Ben knew of Sue's promises, even as he reflected on his own responsibilities to his faith. After prayer and mature discussion, they decided to raise the children as Catholics. Both felt that agreeing on this important issue before marriage made it easier afterward.

Sue and Ben never minimized their challenges. They discussed every objection to their marriage from parents and friends. They read, prayed and sought counsel. As Sue said,

It was our personal maturity and ability to communicate that made the difference. This was especially true at one point in our courtship, when we stopped seeing each other for a while, so that we could sort things out. It was a mutual decision that lasted for about six months, with only an occasional phone call from one or the other asking how each one was doing. After this time, we resumed dating and eventually married. Before marriage, when we decided to raise our children Catholic, we also agreed to go to Mass as a family on Sunday and make the Jewish heritage a complementary part of our family life. We occasionally take the children to the synagogue and observe the religious traditions of both faiths.

Ben also mentioned some of their friends, many of whose mixed marriages ran into serious difficulty. He said,

Many mixed marriages minimize the religious differences between spouses or pretend they do not exist. Important decisions are not faced until they come up. When they arise, the couple often is not prepared to deal with them. One such time is after a child's birth. Frequently, Catholic in-laws want the baby baptized in the Catholic faith. If the other party is Protestant, this side of the family, including the spouse, may want the baby baptized in their church. If the couple experiences conflict over this matter, they sometimes decide not to have the child baptized until later in the child's life. If an interfaith couple fails to address this matter before the child is born, real conflicts can surface. To avoid religious confrontations, some couples stop practicing their faith, leaving children without any faith orientation. This is a big mistake. Finally, with other friends, where one party's faith is stronger than the other's, the stronger faith often takes precedence and the other party resents it.

Sue and Ben believe that addressing the faith issue is one of the most important gifts spouses can give one another and their children. They agreed that "Religious belief is the core and anchor of life. Without it, people flounder, especially in today's amoral society. If children are not taught a faith perspective from early childhood, modern culture imbues them with a secularized religion that leads them away from God. Without God we are nothing."

Ben and Sue's story invites us to ask how couples can create a religious home environment when one spouse is of another faith tradition? Not all spouses are as open, faith-filled or agreeable as Ben and Sue. Many couples about to be married are not religious, and faith is of little or no importance to them. They seldom think about their children's religion and have not progressed very far on their own faith journey. The secular world, time commitments and workloads take them away from serious interest in religious matters.

Many such people feel something is missing, but do not know what it is. They yearn for a stable foundation but do not know where to find it. They get little support from peers. Hence, they wander from day to day, making money, doing their work and enjoying the "American way." They take marriage seriously, but rarely think of making religion a priority. The thought seems foreign to them.

Christian churches need to invite such people to take another look at the components of a happy married life, based on faith in

God. For people entering a mixed marriage, church support has special significance. It can provide the initiative for a change of mind and heart as regards the importance of faith in their marriage. When busy people find something of value for their family in a church setting, they are more inclined to spend time there.

CREATION AND MARITAL LOVE

When Jacob and Traci inquired about my availability to officiate at their wedding, I learned that he was a Muslim, and she was a Roman Catholic. After a prolonged discussion, I agreed to their request. As I met with them in the ensuing months to help them prepare for marriage, I came to see the depths of their love. Both were spiritual, and they sincerely believed that God had blessed their relationship. By praying together, discussing their religious differences and asking God for wisdom, they realized ever more deeply that their love for each other was based on God's love for them.

The Genesis account of creation (1:1—2:4) tells of God's creation of man and woman. It sets the foundation for marriage by focusing on the core relationship between married people. This passage tells us that the love of a man and woman reaches its highest expression in marriage. Their love is rooted in the love God has for them. This reality of divine and human love is the foundation for the Christian teaching on marriage.[18]

The same God who creates spouses out of love calls them to share this love in marriage. The *Catechism of the Catholic Church* describes such love as "the fundamental and innate vocation of every human being...[the couple's] mutual love becomes an image of the absolute and unfailing love with which God loves man. It is good, very good, in the creator's eyes."[19] When an interfaith couple begins their marriage, convinced of these words and the truths that they contain, their marriage can better become a reflection of God's love for them. A focus on love, conveyed during marriage preparation, helps them grow in God's love in spite of their differences.

When the *Catechism* speaks of human relationships, its conclusions about human successes and failures can be applied to marriage. Our disordered human nature, resulting from original and personal sin, sometimes challenges loving marital relationships. Even in the most loving interfaith families, people may offend one another. When spouses fail, God offers them the grace to turn from wrongdoing and seek forgiveness.[20]

CALLED TO SHARE LOVE

To engaged couples he prepares for marriage, Father Stan says, "God's love for you and for your marriage is unconditional. Your free response to God's love as you relate to each other and your family will determine whether or not your marriage will bear fruit."

The tremendous privilege and responsibility of sharing God's love makes humans the stewards of creation. Spouses continue God's creative activity through their love and the blessing of children. When two people marry, they freely set the foundation for the path that their love will take, how it will mirror God's love and how they will share it with others. Seeing their marriage as rooted in such intimate love provides a clearer focus.

Pope Paul VI gives a strong testimony to married love when he says, "Marriage is not, then, the effect of chance or the product of evolution of unconscious natural forces; it is the wise institution of the Creator to realize in mankind His design of love…. For baptized persons, moreover, marriage invests the dignity of a sacramental sign, inasmuch as it represents the union of Christ and the Church."[21]

Pope Paul describes the marks of marital love as fully human, total, faithful and exclusive, and fecund (fruitful). Married love is fully human, because it deepens in the midst of the everyday joys and difficulties, like caring for a sick child or feeling the loss when a son or daughter leaves for college. Such events bring husband and wife into a closer partnership of love and faithfulness, leading them to a deeper union with God and each other. Married love is total, for it is a "a very special form of personal friendship."[22] This friendship moves the partners to eagerly give of themselves for the good of the other, especially during times of sickness and loss. Married love is faithful and exclusive until death. As such, it enables the man and woman to enjoy a deep, enduring and committed relationship all the days of their lives. This often is evident in the great love elderly spouses show to each other, often manifested in a simple smile or glance, rather than in words. Finally, married love is fruitful. It is intended not only for sharing deep, permanent and continuing love between spouses, but also for raising up children for God's glory and the service of humankind. This can become evident when a couple glances at the face of their infant child or shifts their priorities after a child's birth.

CHALLENGES TO A LOVING MARRIAGE

Culture

Jim, a participant in a seminar on the family, addressed the cultural challenges that married couples face. He said, "Everyday events challenge married couples to live righteously. Marriage offers couples unique opportunities to cooperate with God's grace and put children on the right path. Wise married people walk their journey to God by joining with good people everywhere to support upright, moral living. This requires being true to God while reaching out to our neighbor. God's grace helps married couples use God's gifts to build loving families, live good lives, and avoid wrong."

Living an upright life and raising children to follow the right path is not easy in today's cultural climate. Modern society presents many challenges to families. Spouses and children alike never have enough time, often eating and communicating on the run. Family life may change rapidly, requiring adaptation and flexibility. Many parents have little job security and corporate changes sometimes require that a family relocate on short notice. This can separate the nuclear family from their extended families—needed support systems. Violence, life's fast pace, wars and security concerns challenge families and require even closer supervision of children. Life is a buzz of activity, and many married couples feel unsure, fearful and lack hope. Parents have to monitor their children's Internet and television activities. Inappropriate fashions for children and teenagers, misbehaving movie and media idols and an overemphasis on sports give our youth the wrong messages. Often, parents must stand alone against all of these pressures.

Media Images

Married couples find themselves in a world where cohabitating unmarried couples, extramarital affairs, gay unions and abortions are increasingly common. This is reflected and sometimes exaggerated in the media. Addressing the media and mixed marriages, especially those involving a Jewish person, Joan C. Hawxhurst says:

> Some coverage is matter-of-fact, some is skittish and over-simplified. Often it is clear that producers and editors are more concerned about creating a neat, presentable package than about exploring the complexities of life in a mixed marriage. But TV networks, filmmakers and newspapers are starting to pay attention to the fact that much of their audience is directly or indirectly touched by mixed marriage.[23]

The oversimplified media image of mixed marriages offers us an opportunity to focus on what couples really need to hear and believe: All marriages are special. We need to focus on marriage's sacredness and better appreciate what a truly beautiful marriage can be. Engaged and newly married couples need role models and reminders that sacrifice is a vital part of successful marriages. When they find such role models in their families, they can reflect better on what makes their parents' or relatives' marriage blessed.

Spouses
Brad and his fiancée Becca lived in another state and intended to return home to get married. Since Brad had been away since his college days and didn't know any priests, he asked his mother to find one for his wedding. She asked Father Will, who said that he'd talk to Brad when he came home.

Several months later, Becca and Brad visited Father Will. The couple impressed him. Both were mature and serious about their faith. Becca was Presbyterian, Brad Catholic. They had already set limits on how much they would involve their parents in decisions pertaining to their wedding and marriage. They had previously discussed most of the issues that Father Will raised, especially about religion in their home, weekly church attendance and the faith of their children. They communicated well and seemed compatible, basing their love on God and their common faith in Jesus. Their FOCCUS inventory (a premarital inventory for gauging an engaged couple's compatibility) confirmed the priest's intuition that they could work out their faith differences in a mature way.

Becca and Brad viewed their differences as an opportunity to grow in faith. They saw them as blessings, not hindrances. After Father Will explained the covenantal and sacramental nature of their marriage, it was even clearer how their faith in Jesus united them. This awareness allowed them to support each other's faith traditions. They agreed on the faith in which they would raise their children, and both sets of parents affirmed their decision. This couple's approach to marriage illustrates that interfaith couples need to recognize and affirm the core beliefs of their respective faiths. These provide the foundation for their religious growth as a couple. Points of agreement must be acknowledged along with areas of disagreement. When differences are brought to the forefront and understood, it is easier for the couple to clarify misunderstandings and prejudices. The goal is to come to a place where spouses act out of the beliefs they both accept and identify those which only one holds. Most conflicts that Becca and Brad faced before marriage stemmed from denominational differences, not core faith beliefs.

Not all interfaith partners are so blessed as Becca and Brad. Many non-practicing spouses don't mind if their partners practice their faith, but if one spouse is antireligious, or makes fun of the other's faith, problems usually arise. A couple with weak faith often does little about their children's religious formation. They may not have them baptized, or may do so only because of custom or parental pressure. When only one of the partners has deep faith, he or she often attends church events alone. When that spouse also takes the children to church services alone, the children receive a mixed message from their parents.

Some spouses pressure their partners to change faith. This happened to Martha, a strong Catholic. Bill, her husband, was a committed fundamentalist Christian. During their engagement, Bill insisted that they be married in his church. He said that after marriage, Martha could practice her Catholic faith. She went along with his demands.

After marriage, Martha attended the Catholic church for a while, but Bill pressured her to join his church. Feeling trapped, she did. When their first child arrived, he wanted the boy to be enrolled in his fundamentalist church. The pressure increased when Martha told Bill she wished to return to the Catholic church. He became adamant, and she refused to accede to his demands. This division ultimately destroyed their marriage. She told a friend, "I had enough of his fanaticism. I came to resent Bill, as my love ebbed away. I never believed what his church taught and I missed the Eucharist. After I left Bill, I got custody of my son and I plan to raise him Catholic."

DEEP-SEATED ISSUES

Brenda, a Catholic middle-aged woman, married Noah, an active member of the Church of Christ. She reflected on a deeper aspect of the relationship between interfaith couples. She said:

> Often, when dating, deeper, unconscious assumptions never come up between spouses. After marriage, they may begin to surface. Then, a couple needs to examine them and the reasons they believe and act as they do. A simple example of this happened at Christmastime, the first year of our marriage. My family of origin had a tradition of always putting up the Christmas crib and including all the manger's figures on the Sunday before Christmas.
>
> I never discussed this tradition with Noah, but knew he wanted a family crib. On the Sunday before Christmas, I put up a crib that I had purchased. The next morning, something was missing. The wise men were gone. I asked Noah about it. He told me that in his family of origins, they never put the wise men in the crib until the feast of Epiphany. Sensing my disappointment, he returned them to the crib.
>
> The next year, when I put up the crib, I left out the wise men. We discussed the matter and decided to move them around the room indicating their approach to the child Jesus during the entire Christmas Season. Then, on Epiphany, we put them in the crib. We do this every year. When our first child was old enough to appreciate what we

were doing, she moved the wise men closer to the manger each day. This is now one of our important Christmas traditions.

Brenda continued, "Unconscious assumptions, often going back to family beliefs and traditions, surface in different ways. Ellie, a friend of mine, married Max, a non-practicing Jew. He told her it was fine to raise their children as Catholics. This became a real problem for him when he realized after the birth of his son that the boy would never have a bar Mitzvah celebration."

When Rebecca heard Brenda's remarks, she replied, "I, too, am in a mixed marriage. Something similar happened after my marriage. I am an active Baptist and my husband, Clark, is Catholic. As in Brenda's case, I agreed to let Clark raise the children as Catholic. Problems surfaced when our children came. I remember holding and nursing Josh, my first baby, and thinking, 'I really want to pass on to Josh my family's religious traditions. I want to give to my kids what I received.' When that happened, Clark and I prayed about the matter for many months. We eventually reached a resolution to our problem that was sensitive to both traditions. We realized that we had to better understand where each partner's faith came from."

Engaged interfaith couples are wise if they acknowledge their need to continually address faith issues. Growth in faith does not happen overnight. Even when interfaith couples begin marriage with a rudimentary faith, they can commit themselves to its growth. For a couple to stop their faith formation after marriage preparation is unfortunate for them, their children and the faith community.

UNEQUALLY YOKED

A man in a failed mixed marriage said, "Marriage is a partnership, where both spouses pull together. The image of two oxen pulling a cart is applied to married couples in the expression, "equally or unequally yoked." To succeed, both spouses must pull together. When they do not, they are unequally yoked."

Spirituality is the deepest core of the human person and the most powerful binding force of any relationship, especially the marriage of a man and woman. When a couple is equally yoked, based on common spiritual beliefs and practices, it is easier to pull the load. When they are not, it becomes difficult. This is especially the case when one married partner is spiritually active in one's faith and the other is not. Some married couples say this creates a more difficult situation than if spouses belong to different churches but profess common core beliefs.

Mark said that he and his wife, Carole, were baptized Catholics, but she had no interest in her faith and did not practice it. At times, he said, "Carole puts me down for going to church and discourages me from raising the children in the faith. Sometimes, I believe it's harder in my situation than if I had married an active member of another Christian church." It also affects the children. Mark's words indicate that being unequally yoked applies to spouses with the same faith background and to those who belong to different faith traditions. In either case, couples need to consider this serious matter before they marry.

A POSITIVE PERSPECTIVE
Cardinal Walter Kasper affirms the positive side of mixed marriages. He says:

> I assure you that I do not greet those of you today who are in mixed marriages as a "problem," but as people who in your marriages live—in many different ways—a concrete experience, an experience of sharing a covenant between husband and wife which binds you even more deeply in

unity, while at the same time holding something of the painful divisions of Christianity within that unity.[24]

Kasper speaks of families resulting from mixed marriages as communities of life and love, domestic churches, and schools of communion, indicating that "You are not a problem, but you are living in the midst of the serious problem of division within Christianity; in your marriages you have to face this problem daily, and face it with integrity."[25]

Kasper's words encourage couples coming from different Christian traditions to live with faith and integrity, realizing that faithfulness makes significant contributions to the ecumenical movement and church life.[26] Loving families, whose parents belong to different Christian traditions, can keep the ecumenical movement from stagnating, for if they are healthy and vibrant, they bring new motivation into broader ecumenical efforts.[27] To sustain their growth in God's love through family and church relationships, couples need to turn regularly to prayer as individuals and couples, as well as in their family and churches.

FOR REFLECTION

1. Take some time to consider how you and your family spend your time, energy, and resources. What does this inventory indicate about your family's priorities? How do they relate to the importance of religion in your family?

2. What is your attitude toward a Catholic dating someone of another faith or a nonbeliever? Why is this issue not taken more seriously today?

3. How comfortable are you discussing matters of faith with your partner? What serious matters have not been resolved?

4. How does your church or faith community support interfaith couples? What more is necessary?

5. Have you felt "unequally yoked" in your relationship? How can you resolve this with your partner?
6. What are some of the positive possible outcomes of a mixed marriage? When have you witnessed these?

MARRIAGE AS COVENANT AND SACRAMENT

Most

Christian denominations teach that marriage is a serious, covenantal relationship. The Catholic church is unique in its further emphasis on marriage as a sacrament.[28] Because subtle differences exist between the covenantal and sacramental nature of marriage, couples from different faith traditions will benefit from a clearer understanding of these concepts.

In order for a marriage to be valid in the eyes of the Catholic church, both partners must be free to marry and free from other impediments that would invalidate their marriage, intend to enter a lifelong commitment, be open to the possibility of having children and promise to be faithful to each other for life. The Catholic church considers the valid marriage of two validly baptized Christians as a sacramental union. The church does not permit remarriage of a divorced person without a church declaration of nullity of the prior marriage (what is commonly called an annulment).

Affirming the special role of marriage, *Interfaith Families* says:

> The covenant of God and the world as its creative source is given an unsurpassable expression and fulfillment in the covenant of God with Israel and in Christ's spousal relationship to the Church. The baptized join together in marriage as a way of living this covenant that has its origins in

God's love, knowing that the relationship of Christ to the conjugal life of Christians confirms it with the promise of his grace.[29]

SACRAMENTAL GRACES

The covenantal and sacramental nature of marriage are not easy notions to explain. Our idea of covenant comes from the relationship of ancient Israel with God. That covenant bound God to keep the promises made to Abraham and the entire Jewish nation. In return, the Hebrews also were to be faithful—keeping the commandments delivered by Moses, worshiping God alone, making faith the cornerstone of their lives. Jewish marriages were rooted in the covenant bond between God and his people. The marriage ceremony was a solemn event when a Jewish couple pledged faithfulness to each other in marriage, which was a holy union.

During his earthly ministry, Jesus reaffirmed the importance of marriage. His first miracle was at the wedding at Cana. Later, when the Pharisees asked him what reasons for divorce were acceptable, Jesus indicated that the solemn bond between a married couple was indissoluble. Quoting Scripture, he said "[F]rom the beginning of creation, 'God made them male and female.' 'For this reason a man shall leave his father and mother and be joined to his wife, and the two shall become one flesh.' So they are no longer two, but one flesh. Therefore what God has joined together, let no one separate" (Mark 10:6–9). If the covenant between God and the people of Israel was an unbreakable bond, the covenant God makes with the church through Christ is even more profound. Saint Paul directs married couples to embody the same bond and love that Christ has with his church.[30]

In the covenants between God and humans, including the covenant that Jesus made with us through his death and resurrection, God gave us the graces, or helps, to enable us to fulfill our part of the covenant. In our lives, then, God gives us the helps or graces to do good and avoid evil. When Christians marry, they receive in a special way the blessings Jesus won for us on the cross. These graces help them carry out their specific vocations as spouses and parents.

God gives all marriage partners special helps to carry out their marital duties. These graces are given to Christians and all those who marry, as long as they cooperate with the movements of God living within them by sharing an upright life in society and with their spouse and family.

For Christian spouses, however, God gives them special graces as members of his church. By professing a common faith in Jesus, they receive particular helps to communicate Jesus' love with each other and their families. They are to live the life Jesus asks them to live by serving as God's instruments in their families and the world. In a Christian marriage, because spouses profess a common faith in Jesus, they share with others the graces of their baptism in a very specific way through their Christian witness to each other and their children. Just as baptism is a sacrament, so too is marriage a more specified sacrament, rooted in baptism.

The sacrament of marriage focuses the special helps needed to carry out a man's or woman's responsibilities as a spouse and parent. *In this sense, a couple receives the sacramental graces in a way similar to how a priest receives the sacramental graces of orders.* In both cases, the graces help them carry out their special responsibilities. The sacramentality of marriage assures Christian couples that God always will remain faithful to them and give them necessary help to fulfill their marital responsibilities. Just as Jesus' new covenant in his blood is rooted in the covenant first established between God and the Jewish nation, so the sacramentality of marriage is rooted in the covenant relationship that Christian couples begin in baptism.

The concepts of grace and sacramentality can be particularly difficult for those without a Catholic background. Jim, a shopkeeper, offered this story which is pertinent here:

> A young man was hired as a clerk at an ice cream shop. He told the manager how much he loved ice cream and that he knew how to make every kind of sundae, soda and shake. Impressed by his confidence, the manager left the store in the new clerk's care while she ran a short errand. When she returned, she was puzzled to see a long line of customers and her new clerk nearly in tears. "What happened?" she asked. The trembling young man said, "We don't have any ice cream." Enlightened, the manager slid back the huge opaque doors behind the counter, to reveal a freezer filled with every variety. To her satisfaction, the new clerk was able to fill all the waiting customers' orders in a matter of minutes.

Marriage can be compared to this young man's work at his new job. We might be thrilled that we have found a vocation that suits us, that fits our talents, education and aspirations. We might have every confidence in the world that we can fulfill all the demands that will be made of us. But, without grace, we might find ourselves in the same position as the store clerk—lacking the basic resources to meet the challenges ahead.

Those with some familiarity with the church can better appreciate the sacramental nature of marriage by looking at the other sacraments. In each sacrament, we are called to do something well beyond human power. In baptism and Eucharist, we participate in the very life of Christ. Through confirmation we are charged to bring the gifts of the Holy Spirit into the world. Those who are ordained serve in the place of Jesus—celebrating Mass, forgiving sins, counseling those in distress. We are able to fulfill these greater obligations because of the grace God offers through each sacrament. Grace enables us to fulfill our part of the covenant.

Catholics stress the blessings that sacramental graces bring to marriages that are centered in Christ. In referring to these graces, Pope Pius XI said, "By their mutual consent in marriage, the Faithful...open up for themselves a treasure of sacramental grace from which they draw supernatural power for the fulfilling of their tasks and duties faithfully, holily, perseveringly even unto death."[31]

The grace of sacramental marriage is not only a help to preserving the marital union, but also a help to fulfill a spouse's marital and family responsibilities. Each partner is challenged to deepen his or her Christian witness by the intimate daily contact with the other. The natural beauty of marriage is accentuated by giving an example to the world of Christ's love for his church. By striving to be better Christians, the partners become better spouses, and vice versa.

Grace enhances the human will, giving us the ability to do good, even when it is difficult. Grace does not overpower the human will, however. Those who refuse to cooperate with it, who deny it a place in their lives, reap little benefit.

Jake and Marsha were married about five years when their relationship deteriorated. Up to that time, Jake was gone a lot and drank too much, but Marsha tolerated it. But, after getting a new job, Jake started to hang out with some of his buddies after work; he was away from home even more frequently, and he and his friends drank to destructive lengths. In spite of his wife's pleading, Jake refused to get help. In time, his self-destructive path led him to begin an affair with another woman. When a heartbroken Marsha discovered the affair, she prayed for some resolution. Unable to cope with her continued frustration, she finally left Jake.

The graces received in marriage require the cooperation of both spouses. Jake was unwilling to cooperate with the helps God offered him. If one or both married spouses do not cooperate, "...the grace of marriage will remain for the most part an unused talent hidden in a field...." [32] Although these words are addressed to Catholics, they apply to all sacramental marriages. It helps both spouses if they are aware of the graces that their sacramental marriage offers them. These graces can assist them in good and difficult times, help them work out their interfaith differences and strengthen them to fulfill their marital responsibilities.

Pope Paul VI offers a testimony to sacramental marriages in these words, "Christian married couples...must remember that their Christian vocation, which began at baptism, is furthered specifically and reinforced by the sacrament of matrimony. By it husband and wife are strengthened and as it were consecrated for the faithful accomplishment of their proper duties, for the carrying out of their proper vocation even to perfection, and the Christian witness which is proper to them before the whole world." [33]

In confirmation of the wisdom of these words, I recall the large, handmade rosary hanging on my parents' bed for as long as I can remember. A religious brother gave it to my Dad for Christmas years ago. He made it as a thanksgiving gift for Dad's generosity to him over the years. The rosary had no cross on it. For me, this symbolized the many occasions that my Dad and Mom, in the privacy of their room, prayed to God using this rosary, asking for help in difficult situations. They put their own crosses on this rosary, every time they said it. It is a symbol of how Dad and Mom cooperated with the graces that God gave them and our family all the days of their married life.

The *Catechism of the Catholic Church* builds on Paul VI's words about the sacramentality of marriage. It describes Christian marriage as a *Sacrament at the Service of Communion*, which is "directed toward the salvation of others...[it leads to] personal salvation through service to others...and [receive]...particular *consecrations*" through this sacrament.[34] We see these words lived out when spouses sacrifice for each other and their children, and as Christian families reach out to others, especially the poor and needy.

In a similar vein, *Gaudium et Spes* says, "Christian spouses are fortified and, as it were, consecrated for the duties and dignity of their state by a special sacrament."[35] To *consecrate* means "to make holy." Through the sacrament of marriage, a man and woman are made holy. The love they share, including their most intimate relations, are holy symbols of the love that God shares with them and the love they share with each other. Pope John Paul II stresses the sacredness of the marital love of a man and woman in his *Theology of the Body,* which focuses on the goodness of the body itself and how this is brought to fruition in the sacred act of married love.

As mixed marriages between Catholics and baptized Christians increase, with the growing contact of men and women of different races and religions, the Church's teaching on marriage's holiness offers a solid footing for couples from different Christian traditions. This teaching helps them recognize the value of living in accord with the graces that flow from sacramental marriages.

FOR REFLECTION

1. Which stories from the Bible help you recognize God's presence in your family? How do you celebrate this?
2. What is your understanding of grace? When have you felt that God gave you the ability to do something you could not have done otherwise?
3. How does your relationship mirror Christ's relationship with his church? In what ways does it need to grow?

4. For the graces of sacramental marriage to strengthen a couple and their family, the couple needs to cooperate with these graces. What does this mean in your own relationship?

PREPARING FOR AND BEGINNING THE JOURNEY

THE JOURNEY BEGINS

Marriage

is a lifelong journey; it's important to begin well. This means preparing for the journey. In mixed marriages, this preparation focuses one's marriage on faith.

DATING

Prudent couples do not avoid the questions posed by the possibility of marriage when they sense that their relationship is becoming serious. How the couple handles their challenges from the beginning of their friendship is an indicator of how good their marriage will be later on. There are challenges involved in all mixed marriages, and couples need to address them early. It does no good to act as if they did not exist, for religious issues don't go away. Often, it is wise to seek the counsel of parents, married couples in similar circumstances, professional counselors and clergy. An early understanding of the issues at stake will prepare the couple for the road ahead.

ENGAGEMENT

During engagement, interfaith couples must seriously consider the religious issues they have identified in their relationship and focus particularly on those which might affect their children's faith. To testify to religion's importance in the new family, the couple might celebrate their engagement in a more formal way. A priest, rabbi or minister can bless them in a simple engagement ceremony, conducted alone or with loved ones. Alternatively, the couple might ask God to bless their engagement and marriage through a retreat for engaged people or a prayer service that they arrange. Praying together during engagement is an excellent preparation for praying together later on as a family. During engagement a couple can begin habits of prayer, praise and worship that last a lifetime.

During engagement, couples begin to establish patterns for the spiritual environment of their home. In addition to praying together, this means asking for God's help and seeking solid advice on religious issues. Marriage preparation sessions are required by the Catholic church. These sessions help couples learn more about each other's religious beliefs and practices. They should discuss the issue of religious identity in their home, which includes religious prayers, rituals and faith symbols. During this time, couples can clarify what they agree upon, where they disagree and how each can complement the other's religious beliefs without "watering down" their faith as individuals.

It's a challenge to create a home environment that teaches children to respect the religious traditions of their father and mother. A home life rooted in faith is set in motion by a solid spiritual framework before marriage, and is of inestimable value to the couple's deepening commitment and the health of future children. Though children from religious homes sometimes complain about that environment, those who have grown up without religious structure can testify to its importance.

True, many couples have no deep faith or church affiliation. For them, the religious element of their ceremony is secondary to the social dimension of getting married. Some weddings cost more than twenty-five thousand dollars. Many couples will spend months planning for the food, the dress, the decorations, the florist and the photographer. The site for the wedding is, as often as not, chosen for its aesthetic appeal, rather than its significance in the faith life of the couple. At the same time, some couples find marriage preparation sessions an imposition. It makes more sense in our culture to spend months planning for one day, than to spend a few days planning for a lifelong commitment.

I was recently invited to a parish ecumenical meeting which ministers to married interfaith couples. I attended the meeting with about sixteen Catholic and Methodist couples. When asked how they addressed their religious differences, responses included, "The relationship between spouses and God goes together;" "Spouses are obliged to bring each other together in Christ;" "Our mutual relationship with God is central to breaking down our spousal differences;" "Faith happens in relationships;" "The house where we worship is not as important as the faith that we practice;" and, "What we believe is more important than the church we attend." These couples never minimized their religious difference or the challenges involved in attending different churches. Their discussions, however, focused on the conviction that their common core beliefs took precedence over denominational differences.

Most of these couples attended their own churches, but centered their unity as a couple and family on Christ, not their religious denomination. Even when they spoke about their children's church attendance, they stressed that their family's faith in Christ was paramount. Their relationship with Christ was central, and they figured out ways to reinforce it by focusing on common elements in their respective faith traditions. One couple stated, "It's really sad when religion gets in the way of people's relationship with Christ."

A FEW POINTERS

Communicate

All of the participants stressed the need for good communication—it underpinned most of their remarks. They discussed how good communication leads to understanding, which creates a loving environment, where life and faith flourish. One couple said, "To truly encounter God, we must encounter God in loving relationships. How can we really find God, if we are not on the same page with the spouse we love?"

Some participants focused on another theme, suggesting that it is more difficult for a person who marries one with no faith, someone of another faith orientation, or a skeptic, than one who marries a believing Christian of another denomination. They added, "Religion cannot be a divisive element of a marriage or family," and, "A married person with faith and one without faith often is a rocky road." Other attendees indicated the difficulties involved in finding common values in different faith traditions. One woman said, "Shortly after our marriage, we tried to agree on basic beliefs and religious practices. To facilitate this effort, I attended my husband's church and stopped going to the Catholic church. It didn't take long before I missed the Eucharist. When I realized this loss, I returned to the Catholic church. My husband, the great guy that he is, supported me. Now, I am an active parish member along with my children. My husband attends Sunday morning services in his church and Sunday evening Mass each week with our family. Our successful mixed marriage is largely due to our openness with each other, mutual trust, respect and willingness to do the best for each family member. It comes down to the issue of communication."

Communication is central to any happy marriage. This goes deeper than just *talking to one another*. It demands openness to the most intimate details of life, including one's relationship with

God. Usually, in pastoral preparation for marriage, many make a sincere effort to be open. Most are honest about the difficulty of communication, saying that they are making a serious attempt to do so.

It's easy for couples, however, to delude themselves before and after marriage. As a marriage proceeds, this can happen, especially when children come. Then, some parents start communicating with each other through the children. This can be devastating for a marital relationship. When children come into a marriage, the couple can talk and recap the day after the kids go to bed. This helps keep spouses on the same page. Many couples designate times to spend together as a couple outside the home, like going out to dinner weekly. In addition, if arrangements can be made to take care of the children for a weekend, the couple can benefit greatly by making an annual short retreat or day of reflection that centers on communication with each other.

Grow in Faith

If both spouses are religious, they need to discuss their religious beliefs during engagement. When no strong church affiliation exists, they can recommit themselves to their faith. When one partner is an active Catholic and the other is not an active churchgoer, they can grow in faith by praying together or getting involved in social or charitable activities. A couple's faith grows when they do something together to learn about Jesus and his mission. They can volunteer in a homeless shelter or a church. Assisting the poor is an excellent way for couples to recognize their blessings. Pastoral ministers, preparing them for marriage, have to make faith a high priority.

Engaged and married couples are strongly encouraged to spend time praying together. This can take various forms. When going out in the car, they can pray for a safe trip and a good time, centered on God. It helps to put a religious symbol, like a cross or angel, on the sun visor to remind them to do so. Of particular significance is praying together before meals, especially the evening meal. Whether at home or in a restaurant, taking a few moments to recall in silence the events of the day, the blessings received and the gift of love that the couple experiences in each other intensifies their faith and gives strong witness to those about them. To close the day, couples can express gratitude for the day and for the love they share.

When a couple buys a home, whether it is their first or a subsequent one, many pastors encourage them to call the rectory and have the priest or deacon come and bless their home. When they have children, this sends a positive signal to the entire family that where they live is their church of the home, a holy place, with a close connection to the parish.

Raise Children in One Faith Tradition
Most couples in attendance indicated the importance of raising children of mixed marriages in one faith tradition. Their remarks made it clear that the spouses took seriously their religious responsibility to raise their children in a Christian household. Most of the couples raised their children as Catholics. One woman stressed that interfaith couples "need to have the family together worshipping in one church." Another said, "It's important for a family to go together to one church." Two families, who raised their children as Catholics, mentioned that several of their children left the Catholic church and joined other denominations after they married. They indicated that they were better able to appreciate such decisions because of their own experiences.

When the topic turned to the family environment, a participant remarked, "At home, it's important for us to stress common elements of both faiths. We do this in prayer and simple rituals that surround religious feasts and seasons. Doing so hasn't weakened our different religious traditions or led our children into relativistic religious beliefs. We clarified, as soon as possible, the differences between our children's Catholic faith and the Methodist faith that their father practices. My husband and I try our best, but it's not easy."

Just as Jesus called the disciples to evangelize "all nations"[36] so he calls each Christian parent to educate their children in the ways of faith. Parents have the major responsibility to do this. For this to happen, they must trust in God's guidance and agree upon basic Christian teachings. They can use the Bible and Christian stories as the foundation of teaching their children. Before children are born, parents have to choose the denomination the children will embrace. As children are initiated into the faith that the parent choose for them, parents can explain the beliefs of both partners, but not introduce conflict and ambiguity into the child's faith. They can stress common core Christian beliefs. In this process, parents need to help children clarify their own identity, as they integrate elements from their parents' religious traditions.

Confirming what these couples have indicated, the spouse with the strongest faith usually has the greatest influence on the faith of the family. It is important for couples to agree on the faith which their future family will practice. In filling out church papers, the Catholic party must promise to do his or her best to have the children baptized and raised in the Catholic faith. Some other denominations place a similar obligation on their members. Insistence from both spouses that the family practices his or her religion often portends problems.

Resolving these important issues can indicate a deep spirituality, showing that one is willing to set aside personal preferences for the greater good. Jim, a nonpracticing Protestant, married Millie, a Catholic. For forty years, Jim maintained a healthy attitude toward his wife and their seven children's Catholic faith. He encouraged Millie to have the children baptized. He often attended the Catholic parish and supported the family's Catholic home environment. Jim came to the children's sacramental celebrations and sent them to Catholic schools. He never became Catholic, but his positive attitude set a solid example for this family.

Before marriage, children's faith, education, family prayer and worship patterns need to be addressed. So does a couple's way of handling in-laws who disagree with their decisions, especially in faith matters.

Understand the Impact of Our Diverse Culture

The couples commented perceptively on the wider ecumenical culture where we live. One said, "People today are more prone to enter mixed marriages because the world where they are born, raised, go to school and work is ecumenical. We meet people of different religious and ethnic backgrounds everyday. In this climate, it's natural that people fall in love with those of different faith traditions. We must get used to living this way. This will motivate us to pass on beliefs and values to our children that help them thrive in the modern world."

Picking up on the theme of an ecumenical culture, another participant chimed in, "Young people, living in such a climate, don't think twice about dating and falling in love with someone of another faith. It was different when I was young. In one sense, the present climate of tolerance doesn't present as critical a challenge to married couples as the culture when I grew up. But, on the other hand, the challenges are greater, because parents and pastoral ministers do not really know how to give good guidance to those coming along. It's like our discussion tonight. Things are up in the air, for we're still learning about ourselves. Life is too fluid and the pace is too fast. Hopefully, we will soon be able to give young people a better roadmap, helping them to cope with challenges that mixed marriages present."

In response, an elderly participant said, "I understand why about 40 percent of Catholics marry non-Catholics. I'm waiting to see how the larger church addresses this challenge. Most churches offer couples pretty good marriage preparation, but what they provide is not adequate in today's world. Much more is required to help engaged couples face the serious challenges before them. We need to invite more successful interfaith couples to counsel those about to enter mixed marriages. Even after marriage, parishes need to offer more spiritual support to mixed marriages during the early years, especially when children come along."

Social pressures and a materialistic lifestyle often dictate a family's basic orientation, if parents fail to give priority to family relationships. Without a firm commitment to put family first, the challenges coming at families from all sides can substitute for more prudent family choices.

A couple needs to do their best to live from the heart of their relationship. This means acting according to their beliefs, rather than allowing themselves to be pushed around by outside forces that interfere with their personal and family relationships. Parents have to prioritize their children's time, lest sports and childhood activities become the major driving forces of family life. It's important for parents to monitor children's television and computer use from the beginning and provide good educational resources and opportunities.

Remember That the Initiative Comes From God

After a prolonged discussion, a middle-aged woman said, "The initiative for a loving marriage and family comes from God, not the spouses. Faith tells us that God directs our lives. Why did I meet and fall in love with my spouse? Why is our family blessed? The Christian faith believes that every hair of our heads is numbered and known by God. God plays a part in our coming together and staying together. Hence, we are wise to center our lives on God."

This woman's words reflect her deep faith and trust in God. In a world where we depend largely on personal initiative and talents, trusting in God more than our own efforts, is not easy. It requires constant growth in faith and the willingness to set aside time every day to remember the God who created us and keeps us in existence. Without a solid prayer life it is difficult to maintain trust in God's providential care when we are challenged and discouraged. In life's joys and troubles, spouses need to remember that God's grace is always present, directing them in the right path.

Put Marital Success in God's Hands

"A marriage's success is more in God's hands than ours," stressed one interfaith couple. They said, "We depend too much on our efforts and forget God. In saying this, we do not imply that we don't have to work at our marriage. Our efforts are essential. They begin with our attitudes toward one another. Nonetheless, anything we do is rooted in something deeper. This is God's love and providence. When we put our marriage in God's hands, it becomes easier to recognize how we need to turn to God for wisdom in our marriage and family."

Couples coming from different Christian traditions need to have faith in one another and in their common path to God. Every road has obstacles, and when a couple sees marriage as the one road they both travel together, they can face the obstacles that their religious differences present. They look to the goal of the quest, which is happiness in this life and in eternity for themselves and their family. Keeping the goal in mind helps put in better focus what they must do to reach it. This helps some couples make religious differences strengths, not weaknesses. As a middle-aged couple emphasized, "Above all, couples need to maintain faith in one another and not allow religious differences to become wedges between themselves on their common path with God."

Remember That Love Is About Others in Christ
A middle-aged woman said, "Love is about others, not ourselves. No room exists for destructive competition in a marriage." She stressed that in our self-centered society it's hard for married couples to be other-centered when it comes to marriage. Each spouse must be open to the other person and show signs of deep love. A couple's love and affection for each other can be one of the best gifts they give their children. When this happens, the children grow up in a healthy environment. In mixed marriages, such love extends to supporting the spouse in his or her faith and church affiliation. Through mutual love, spouses help each other grow in their mutual love, and in love of God, family and neighbor. Some parents are able to be selflessly dedicated to their children, while taking their spouses for granted. This can only lead to problems for the couple and their entire family.

A young Catholic mother said, "Spouses are obliged to bring each other together in Christ. My love for my spouse is more about our relationship with each other in Christ than about the church we attend. Love is the communication channel between God and us. We love each other because God's love dwells within us. It is this love that we share with ourselves, our children, and friends."

Most couples at the meeting attend their own churches, but center their unity as a couple and a family on Christ, not their religious denomination. Their relationship with Christ is central and they figure out ways to reinforce it by focusing on common faith elements in their respective faith traditions.

Maintain Hope

A Methodist woman in a mixed marriage offered wise advice when she said, "Interfaith married couples need to remember that Christianity is a religion of hope. In our spousal and family relationships, we often reflect this hope. This is important today, when little hope exists in the world. The fact that we know God is with us and will never abandon us is a reason for hope. We need to remind family members of this, particularly when things do not go well. I don't know where I'd be today, if I didn't have hope. I find it a privilege to share it with my spouse and family."

Recognize Personal Problems

Jim is a popular tenured professor. His outstanding qualities are apparent. Often, he eats lunch with several colleagues. During these luncheons, Jim doesn't talk much about his personal life. Most of his colleagues know only that he lives with his two sons. He is a faithful Catholic, attends daily Mass and serves as a Eucharistic minister. While Mark, one of Jim's lunch partners, was conducting a seminar on Catholic marriage practice for engaged and married couples, he asked Jim's advice. Jim said,

> I am divorced from my wife, who was not Catholic. We split up because of personal, not religious differences, even though our different religions often were matters of contention. The real issue focused on our personal problems. She was highly insecure, possessive and uncontrollable if she didn't get her way. I was stubborn. Some friends said that I was not as troubled as she was, but her problems accentuated mine. We should have recognized the caution signals before marriage, but we were too infatuated to think clearly.
>
> In conducting your seminar, concentrate on the fact that when things go really wrong in a mixed marriage, often deep

personal issues, more than religious ones are involved. Such personal problems are more basic than differences in faith. If my former wife and I had been mature and stable, we probably could have worked out the religious issues. Over time, differences in faith became indicators of our personal problems and inability to see one another's viewpoint. After our divorce, I turned to prayer and professional counseling for help. Today, I am a more mature and whole person.

Jim's advice contains an important suggestion for interfaith couples. In any marriage, the couple's personal compatibility is more basic than their religious orientation. In successful marriages, regardless of cultural and religious differences, the couple's ability to get along with each other is the most critical factor.

After reading Jim's story, Father Ted, an experienced pastor, said that he has dealt with a number of Catholics or Catholics married to people of other faith traditions who divorced not long after their marriage. He attributes many of these marital failures to not addressing their deeper relational or family issues prior to marriage.

Face Issues Honestly
The religion of the other party often is not a major issue for many interfaith couples when they begin dating. If the time comes to seriously consider marriage, it may become one. At this point, couples rarely break off relationships because of religious differences. Instead, some avoid the matter. This never works, for differences must be addressed. Few engaged or married couples want to address challenges that interfere with their relationship. Often, they avoid them, hoping problems will go away. The following case illustrates this point.

Jane suspected that Ed, her fiancé, was unfaithful to her during their engagement. She hesitated to confront him, unwilling to accept that this was happening. After marriage, Ed's infidelity continued, as did her denials. When his behavior became public, they divorced.

It's not much different when a person drinks too much, takes drugs or is overly possessive. Marriage does not change a person's personality. What people are before marriage, they remain afterward. The same is true of interfaith issues that a bride or groom suspect will cause problems after marriage. These may involve the family's religion, children's faith, time spent in church activities or the faith of the other spouse.

In speaking about the challenging issue of the faith in which children are to be raised, Edna, a woman in a mixed marriage said,

> I have seen many times the situation where a person says before marriage that he or she doesn't care about religious differences. Then, after children are born, this spouse has strong feelings that the children should be raised in his or her faith and traditions.
>
> A Christian colleague of mine married a non-practicing Muslim who agreed that the kids could be raised Christian. They had two children who were raised Christian for ten years. Then, the husband visited his dying father, who made him promise to convert his wife to Islam. He agreed. When his wife refused, and said this was not their premarriage agreement, he divorced her.

During engagement, if either person seriously suspects that their upcoming marriage will cause serious problems and not work, the couple may have to end their relationship. Ideally, both partners should concur in such a decision, but sometimes this does not happen. After marriage, domestic violence, adultery and other serious matters often lead to separation or divorce. When such issues arise, the couple ought to seek advice from a professional counselor, pastor, family member or friend.

In a graduate marriage class, a student gave the results of a research study of successful marriages that lasted over thirty years. The data indicated that no single pattern exists for the success of these marriages. In some marriages, one spouse made most of the decisions. Their communication happened in this light and the couples were happy. These marriages met the couple's needs. In other marriages, the parties communicated in a more dialogical way, expressed great love to their family and shared responsibility for family decisions. They were open and up-front with their spouses. Some were outgoing, others were quiet. Most were comfortable with their spouses. In still other marriages, the couple's communication was uneven, but they got along most of the time. Some were boisterous with each other, yet they maintained no hard feelings afterward. This research study seems to indicate the differences that existed among successful married couples and the difficulty of coming up with criteria to predict success after marriage. Although the data didn't say so, many couples seem to look unconsciously for a spouse that mirrors psychological aspects found in their family of origin.

No one can predict the outcome of marriages. Some marriages that seem to be sure things, fail. Others that appear shaky at first, succeed. Marriages require constant effort. In forty-five years of preparing couples for marriage and officiating at their ceremonies, the outcome of many marriages has surprised me.

Even though no marriage's outcome can be predicted, marriage preparation must look to the significant personal and interpersonal factors that affect a marriage's success or failure. These have to do with a person's physical, psychological and spiritual state. For this reason premarital inventories, like FOCCUS, provide valuable data that enables couples to look seriously at their relationship. In mixed-marriage preparation, it does little good to stress differences in a couple's faith if personal problems are not addressed.

FOR REFLECTION

1. What is the single most important element of your upcoming wedding? When making wedding preparations, how can you keep faith a priority?

2. What are the major challenges newly married couples face today? How might a couple from different faith traditions be better equipped to meet those challenges? How might their differences be a hindrance?

3. When is it too soon to discuss the faith life of future children? When is it too late?

4. Should religious disagreements be handled differently than conflicts over other issues? Why or why not?

5. Do you think that what a couple believes is more important than the church they attend? Why or why not?

6. To what extent do you believe that the success of mixed marriages is in God's hands? In the couple's hands?

7. To what degree do you believe that the strongest point of unity for interfaith Christian couples can be found in their relationship with each other centered on their mutual belief in Christ?

THE WEDDING CEREMONY

The

wedding ceremony is a culmination and a beginning. It culminates the couple's meeting, getting to know each other, falling in love, deciding to marry, engagement and preparing for marriage. It begins their married life and hope for a happy family. Like other significant rituals, it touches their deep core and invites family and friends to celebrate their joy and happiness.

The secular, functional aspects of a wedding often assume greater significance than the religious rite itself. Society imbues couples with materialistic values, which they unconsciously assimilate into their marriage. The wedding dress, flowers, photos, church aisle's length, rehearsal dinner and reception often take center stage. Even though such matters may have to be decided well in advance of a wedding, the couple has to take seriously the spiritual aspects of getting married. A prime example of how these two go hand-in-hand: Some couples pick the date they want and reserve a hall for the reception, only to discover that the parish church is not available at that time. While it is true that God is always available to us, the resources and staff of any parish are limited. As in all areas of life, it is a good practice to put God first and everything else will fall into place. Reserve the church first, and make your plans from there.

WHERE CAN THE COUPLE GET MARRIED?

If the Catholic partner has regularly attended his or her parish church, that should be the obvious choice. Many churches require parish membership for those wishing to be married there; some offer the venue for free to parishioners, but charge a fee for others. A phone call to the rectory will answer your questions on this matter.

If the Catholic partner has been away from the parish (off to college, for example, or working in another locale), but wishes to marry in the family's parish, a family member can make the necessary inquiries. A Catholic who has been away from the faith altogether might have more challenges. The pastor of the church in which you wish to marry will encourage you to become reacquainted with the faith as you pursue your marriage preparation. Anyone connected with the church will impress upon you the seriousness of the commitment you are about to make, and the commitment you have already made to Christ and his church through your baptism. This can be a wonderful time of rediscovering the joy and privilege of being Catholic. A closer relationship with God can only prepare you to be a better spouse.

A couple should contact the parish in which they wish to be married as early as possible. Generally, a preparation period of at least six months is necessary. You will be invited to speak to a priest or deacon about the wedding. Catholic persons not marrying in their home parish will need to know where they were baptized—a baptismal certificate is required. The person conducting the interview will ask some questions to determine whether the parties are "free to marry" and free of any impediments. There are some basic considerations—you cannot marry a close blood relative, you must have at least two witnesses, and there are minimum age requirements (most of these are also state laws). If either person has been previously married, whether or not in a

Catholic ceremony, there may be obstacles to your union. Some can be overcome (if, for example, the marriage can be declared null due to "lack of canonical form" or some other defect), but some cannot. The priest or deacon can advise you on a course of action, depending on your particular situation (see Canons 1083–1094).

Pre-Cana

Most parishes require couples to attend marriage preparation classes, sometimes called pre-Cana classes (from the biblical story of the wedding at Cana). These can be sessions with the priest or other parish minister and the couple over a course of months. They can also take other formats. Faith issues will be discussed, but the person conducting your classes will also help you consider other important issues—how the two of you handle important decisions about work, money and family relationships, for example. Most couples find this experience thought-provoking and rewarding.

Planning the Liturgy

The parish staff will also help you plan your ceremony. An important perspective to keep in mind is that, in the Catholic view, marriage is about more than the couple—it is an important event that concerns the parish community. Rather than thinking of this viewpoint as detracting from "your day," let it be a sobering reminder of all the lives that will be permanently changed as a result of your wedding. One parishioner commented to me that this concept really struck her when she was organizing photos of family members from generations gone by. "I saw the aged-stained photograph of my great-grandparents in their wedding clothes. They looked happy, but also very serious. Then I realized that the entire box of photos from which I had taken that one picture were all of people (including me) that never would have been born if my great-grandparents hadn't gotten married—

literally hundreds of human lives can trace their beginnings to that moment."

Each church will have a slightly different way of deciding who selects the music and who plans the liturgy. Some couples like to have more choices. Others are disappointed that they cannot have their ceremony in a park or play their favorite song during Communion. Any wedding certainly offers plenty of other opportunities to personalize the ceremony to fit the couple's taste.

Most weddings of two Catholics take place within the context of Mass (this accounts for the "long Catholic wedding" some of your non-Catholic friends may speak about). Dioceses often do not permit mixed marriages to be celebrated within Mass without permission of the bishop. One reason for this is that the non-Catholic spouse (and all other non-Catholics in attendance) cannot receive Communion. This can emphasize the division within the families at a time where unity should be the prevailing theme.

MARRYING IN ANOTHER CHURCH

If the couple has decided to marry in the non-Catholic's church, the Catholic party will still need a dispensation from canonical form to do so. Because such requests have become more common, these dispensations are more easily obtained now than in times past, but it is still not a trivial matter. Be sure to contact your parish at the earliest possible date to let the priest know of your wishes. He can advise you of the steps to take.

MARRYING OUTSIDE THE CHURCH

A Catholic who marries outside of the Catholic church, such as in a civil ceremony or in a Protestant church and without proper dispensation, is not—to put it bluntly—"married" in the eyes of the church. Although this was once common knowledge among Catholics, it is less so now. There are remedies within the church for such marriages. The spouses must make a new act of consent when they have their marriage convalidated by the church. To begin the convalidation process, it is best to contact a priest (or someone he has chosen) to discuss the situation.

PREVIOUSLY MARRIED

As we already indicated, a central issue that your parish priest or deacon will ask about is whether both parties are free to marry. If either person has been previously married (and the former spouse is still living)—even in a "lack of canonical form" case such as the one described above—this must be disclosed. The particulars of their case must be submitted to the local marriage tribunal, which much issue a "declaration of nullity" before a Catholic marriage can take place. No Catholic should avoid this process. It can be difficult for anyone to reconsider a failed relationship, but the process required by the tribunal is necessary to determine if the couple is free to celebrate a Catholic marriage. There are some costs associated with this step, but no one is denied access to the tribunal for lack of ability to pay. (For further information about the tribunal process, see *Catholics, Marriage and Divorce: Real People, Real Questions*, by Victoria Vondenberger, Cincinnati: St. Anthony Messenger Press, 2003).

If the tribunal issues a declaration of nullity, this does not change the civil aspects of your former marriage. Any children you may have had will still be "legitimate." You will still be liable by your former partner for any settlement ordered by the state in your divorce or dissolution proceedings, and of course, you will still be legally and morally obligated to care for your children.

Not every marriage that fails can be declared null. If the tribunal rules "against" you, do not hastily dismiss its assessment. Little can be gained from fleeing one failed relationship and rushing into another marriage. Give yourself and those you care about the time to process your past. If your valid marriage is not declared null by the church, you will not be free to marry in the church in the future. Seek spiritual advice and counseling. Pray. The Catholic church is a staunch defender of marriage, sometimes even long after one or both of the spouses have given up on it.

Develop Good Habits

While you are planning your wedding, you are encouraged to make regular church attendance a priority, especially if it has not been so in the past. If there are other parish groups that interest you, consider those as well.

The first years of marriage are a delicate balance of developing your own identity and the identity you share with your spouse as members of a new family. If both these identities are solidly grounded in faith, the two of you are more likely to grow together as the years pass than to grow apart.

For Reflection

1. What were your expectations of your wedding day and marriage while you were growing up? How have they changed? What role does your faith play in those expectations?
2. Ask your partner to describe his or her ideal wedding ceremony and marriage. How does this vision differ from your own?
3. Do you have difficulty arriving at decisions about marriage preparation and wedding plans with your partner? What does this suggest about your ability to communicate with one another? How do you resolve conflicts?
4. Many couples express the sentiment that they will be glad when the wedding is over. Do you share this feeling? How do you see your wedding day as a beginning rather than an end?

CREATING A FAMILY IDENTITY

PERSONAL AND FAMILY IDENTITY

The telephone called me to attention on a cold December morning at 5:37 AM. While fumbling to answer it, I already knew its message. In a few seconds, a gentle voice confirmed my fears. A nurse from St. George Hospital said simply, "At 5:10, Stanley Hater, your father, died peacefully. When the orderly came into the room, not a sheet was ruffled."

A panorama of emotions and memories filled me. I remembered the good times, and how Dad sacrificed for our family. Hurriedly, I called my sister, went to her home, and we proceeded to Mom's house. When we rang her doorbell, she answered in her nightgown, looked at us, and said, "Oh, Stanley died." Mom knew, we didn't have to tell her.

We remained silent as we led Mom into the living room and sat beside her on the couch. Tears gently flowed down her cheeks, as she prayed. Then, Mom looked at the crucifix on the wall and worriedly said, "What will I do? Stanley, my husband of forty-four years, is gone. Now, I am only half a person."

We put our arms around her and answered, "Mom, we need you; you must go on. You have to live for us." Exhausted from waiting on my father day and night, Mom closed her eyes and slept for five hours. After Dad's burial, Mom lived twenty-two more years, was a wisdom figure, and inspired her children, grandchildren and great grandchildren. She was young until the day she died at 91 and blessed us through her faith and dedication.

PERSONAL IDENTITY

Identity involves recognizing who you are as a person and part of a group. It is a quest that strives to relate the deepest core of my being with my gifts, aspirations, tasks and responsibilities. The goal of this search is to discover my role as a person and a member of a group. Identity is closely associated with a sense of belonging. As authors Petsonk and Remsen say, "Identity is not what you believe: it's where you belong."[37] A sense of belonging helps us better understand our place in the world.

To discover who you are, it helps to begin with your personal story. Where did you come from? Who were your parents and family? What is your ethnic background and faith tradition? What cultural factors influenced you as you matured? What are your moral and religious values? How did successes and failures affect you personally? What are your present responsibilities and future aspirations? Such questions connect with a deep dimension of your identity.

Analyzing identity moves us beyond the functional world of money, work, pleasure and success to the deeper recesses of our person to the core dimension of who we are. In so doing, we enter a spiritual realm and ask questions more profound than, "Should we move to a bigger home in the suburbs?" or "What clothes should we wear to the concert?" Rather, we address core issues like, "Is there a God?," "What are our responsibilities before God?," "Why were we born?," "What is the meaning of life?," "Are our moral values consistent with our religious beliefs?," "What will happen when we die?" and "How do the above questions relate to my identity—who I am?"

Without addressing such core questions, you cannot adequately consider the identity issue of who you are as a person or group member. Even when identity concerns your role in a functional group, like a financial team, ultimate core issues set the foundation for your decisions and influence how you treat members of the group. Without addressing those core issues, what you do and how you do it remains clouded. If this is true in life generally, it is especially true in mixed marriages.

DEVELOPING IDENTITY

It is helpful to remember that identity, the search for who we are and our life's role, is a process, not a product. Our identity shifts focus as time passes and circumstances change. While the core of our being stays the same, we change with age and experience. We assume new responsibilities and let go of old ones. When asking about the identity of a married couple as a couple or the identity of a particular family, it is better to think in terms of a work in progress, not a finished product.

Coming from the core of who we are as persons, each individual has inherent dispositions, given to us as natural gifts by birth. We mold these through interchange with our parents, siblings, friends, neighbors, creation and work associates. These provide an initial blueprint for our race, color, sexual orientation, personality, temperament and other physical and mental characteristics. How we shape them throughout life affects who we are and what we become.

To adequately address our identity we need to connect with the core of human life. We find clues to our identity by considering core issues, like why we were born, how we live and what is our final destiny, rather than by looking at our ability to make money, speak well or receive earthly honors.

A sense of identity gives a person an anchor in life. When a child grows up without being rooted deeply in a home, understood in a psychological, geographic and religious sense, it may be difficult to feel connected on a deeper level. In other words, "People who are raised without a clear sense of religious belonging may feel a void in their lives."[38] Drawing upon a series of interviews and their professional experiences, Petsonk and Remsen "...have come to feel it is not satisfactory to raise a child with no group identification, no experience of belonging."[39]

Connection with a faith tradition gives a child security and a sense of who they are in a broader religious context. For this reason, the above authors ".....recommend that you give [a child] a clear grounding in a specific tradition."[40] Throughout their treatment, Petsonk and Remsen claim that children raised with an identity in one faith often are more secure than those brought up in two different traditions. They say that a single tradition is "tied to some practices, some values, and a community of people with whom [the child] is familiar."[41] Even though different ethnic, cultural and personal gifts of spouses enhance a child and a household, a child's religious orientation in one faith tradition needs to be clear. If not, some children may conclude that they have multiple religious identities.

Petsonk and Remsen imply that raising children in two different faith traditions is confusing to children. Many—but not all—psychologists, ministers and parents agree. Couples should consider this issue, for every maturing child passes through stages of personal and identity development. It is hard enough for children to sort out who they are in one faith tradition. It is doubly difficult if the children are floating between two different religious identities on their way to maturity.

Relationships clarify personal identity. This begins at birth and lasts a lifetime. At birth, children do not acknowledge themselves as individuals. They initially become aware of other people and events, which become mirror images in a child's developing sense of self. Through the give-and-take of acceptance and rejection, usually from parents, children gradually develop a notion of themselves. The way they are treated influences their self-image. Children who receive love and affection from parents develop a different idea of themselves than children who are rejected. Many other factors can affect identity, too. This can happen at school when peers ridicule a child, at home when siblings reject a brother or sister, and in social situations when children are mocked by their peers. Childhood abuse and neglect affect physical and mental well-being and can alter a child's spiritual sense and personal identity.

IDENTITY BEFORE GOD

All early peoples had recourse to higher powers to answer core life questions. They based their beliefs on a communal faith, which grounded them as a believing people and pointed beyond themselves to a greater power. They believed that a divine plan governed the universe. Their sacred writings described the designs of God or their gods, addressed deep mysteries and shed light on the destiny of believers. They looked to a transcendent realm beyond themselves and to a core level within themselves to unlock their true identity.

Christians believe that one, true God reveals our ultimate destiny in the Hebrew and Christian Scriptures. Jesus' life, teaching, suffering, death and resurrection give our quest for identity its greatest clarity. Jesus taught us who we are before God, and how to live. Jesus promised that if we live by God's plan, we will enjoy heaven's happiness forever. We learn from him that to oppose God's designs means living in an incomplete, ambiguous and sinful world. Such an existence makes it impossible to know our identity as sons and daughters of God. In Christian marriage, this means that the deepest identity of spouses is found in their covenantal and sacramental union in Christ. Their love becomes one with God's love, revealed in Christ. They are one, as he is one with the Father and Holy Spirit and with his entire body, the church.

We must take our search deeper than our work, friends and family. We connect with our inner core. The Holy Spirit, dwelling there, encourages us to love God, spouse, neighbor and self. Without connecting with God, present in our inner core, we cannot reach our final destiny. Healthy personal, spousal and family identity also includes the acknowledgment of core issues like trust, forgiveness, love, compassion and hope. These are especially important for interfaith spouses, who have different religious values and beliefs.

If a couple differs in ethnic or cultural background, problems are magnified even more. It is difficult for a couple to become a "we," if they radically differ in their most fundamental beliefs.

The identity issue looms large in families where one member is not Christian. If the couple's religious patterns differ radically, they need to sort out areas of agreement and disagreement. If relationships clarify our personal and family identity, but spousal relationships differ in religious beliefs, where does this leave marriage and family identity? How, for example, does a couple, one of whom is Catholic and the other Hindu, identify at their core, when their religious orientations differ so drastically?

Relational Identity
Relational identity is a person's identity within a group. Throughout history, the group often has been more important than the individual. Before modern times, relational identity took precedence over individual identity. Such relational identity focuses on this innate need for community. In biblical times, the Hebrew people gave priority to the nation, not the individual. God established a covenant with the Hebrew people and promised salvation to them. They were his chosen people. Jesus called disciples and established a community to carry on his work. Native Americans place high priority on their tribe. Some ethnic

groups depend on clans for protection, food and shelter. Relational identity takes various forms. Some men and women develop relational identity within religious communities. High school athletes, while playing school sports, find identity with other team members. A functional relational identity exists between business associates, who develop ways to market products. In all life, we enter relationships that define our identity within a group.

At the beginning of this chapter I told a story about my father's passing. When my mother said she was half a person, she indicated how her spousal relationship had shaped her personal identity. Spousal identity of a husband and wife, from which family identity springs, is a most fundamental kind of relational identity. In one way or another, relational identity is always associated with community. Many spouses do not depend heavily on their partner for their personal identity, as my mother depended on my Dad for hers. Other spouses may depend too heavily on their spouse for their religious identity. Regardless of the personal autonomy that spouses maintain after marriage, each person's individuality shifts throughout life.

The book of Genesis hints at the importance of a shared married life when it says that a man and woman become one in marriage. It begins a new relational identity for them and their children. Such identity differs from their personal identity before or . after marriage.

In dealing with relational identity, it is helpful to distinguish between spousal and family identity. Spousal identity is the identity of a married man and woman, discovered in relationship with each other. Family identity refers to the identity of the family as a whole and each family member as part of a specific family group. Both kinds of identity vary in intensity, depending on the spousal relationship or family in question.

Kim and Brian, married for ten years, have developed a deep, intimate spousal identity. They mutually decide the best course of action in family affairs, religious practices and work. Their marital relationship helps them identify who they are as a loving couple. Their communication is good, and they make decisions in mutual trust, even though Brian is Lutheran and Kim is Catholic. Their three children are their top priority. Their nine-year-old child goes to a Catholic school. Their three- and six-year-old children have been baptized in the Catholic faith. Kim is fulfilling her promise to do all in her power to raise her children in the Catholic faith. Brian agreed to do so before they were married. He often attends Mass with the family, before he goes to his Lutheran service. The Catholic faith is an aspect of who they are as a family, even though Brian practices his Lutheran faith.

This family decides on many things as a small community. They agree on how to spend their Sundays, where to go on vacation and how to share household responsibilities. They set Sunday aside as their family day. The family attends church in the morning, does fun things in the afternoon and eats dinner at home in the evening. Those who know them recognize that their actions and attitudes help constitute their family identity. This couple's and family's identity includes a commitment to spending significant time with each other.

Other couples and families live more functional lives. They may hardly see one another daily and commit little time to deepening their relationship. Sometimes they give a higher priority to furthering their professional career. Such an attitude affects their children, who may learn from them that functional things are more important than deep relationships. Still other spouses may subjugate their spousal relationship too much to their children's lives by trying to maintain a hectic schedule of children's activities, and not taking sufficient time as a couple. This, too, may reflect negatively on them and their children. Each married couple and family develops a particular spousal and family identity. Some are deeper and more lasting than others. Whatever the case, people's identity affects the way they live.

We learn our true identity through others. Such knowledge begins in God, who gives us a glimpse into who we are, when we learn more about God and ourselves. We learn about God through the words and example of others. Good people teach us that God is present in our experiences. Association with such people shapes our personal identity. Since human interchange clarifies identity, each spouse plays a vital role in developing the partner's identity.

My family celebrates our family relational identity as we page through old family picture albums. Snapshots of Dad and Mom's teenage years precede their wedding pictures. Examining them, we learn how our family changed, as children came, vacation trips happened, and household gatherings became more prominent. When looking at the pictures, we observe our parents growing older, the family maturing and new members entering our household. In so doing, we remember the stories told by my father. While still living, he often sat with us and described events surrounding the pictures, including the family store, 1937 flood and our move to a new home. Through such pictures and stories, we reinforce our family relational identity.

After Mom and Dad's death, we continue to recount family stories and reexamine the old pictures. They help us better appreciate the centrality of the Catholic faith to our family attitudes and activities. We recall the family picnics in the park, the high school football game, graduations, vacations, family meals, working together on home projects, the flower and vegetable garden, and trips to our relatives' homes. We also remember religious rituals of baptism, first communion, confirmation, religious pageants, May crowning, statues, sacred images in the home, seminary days, convent pictures, church marriages and Sunday Mass attendance. Reflecting on them, we realize how much our family environment affected our self-image. Dad and Mom spent many years alone and with their children, as a compatible team. No wonder that Mom described herself the way she did after Dad died!

How to create family identity, when the basic beliefs of the spouses differ, is an issue that couples in mixed marriages need to consider. Both spouses must address relational family identity as a whole, their spousal identity, and their personal identity.

The religious identity of interfaith families, taken as a unit, differs from the personal religious identity of husband or wife. The relational identity of any Christian interfaith family includes an ecumenical dimension. Even though the parents raise their children as Catholics, the family as a whole includes a member of another Christian faith tradition, whose religious practices are part of the family's relational identity.

IDENTITY AND MARRIAGE

Most people strive to develop a healthy balance when they consider marriage, family and career. They instinctively sense the priority of spousal and family relationships. Not all people, however, accept these priorities. Take the case of a man in an undergraduate religion class. He strongly disagreed with most classmates who said one's career was secondary to the relationship with a spouse and children. He replied, "No! I first plan to succeed in business. After this happens, I will give priority to my wife and children." Another student pointed out that with this philosophy, his wife and children might leave him by the time he becomes successful.

Reflecting similar thoughts, a woman in a seminar on career opportunities said, "After marriage, I intend to maintain a strong personal autonomy, rather than give priority to the relationship with my husband. He feels the same way. Because we have different career paths, we will live in separate cities and get together about once a month. Maybe, someday, we'll have kids." Such success-oriented attitudes are more common than one realizes. Increasingly, married couples live independent lives, even under the same roof. Society's individualism often makes it difficult for married couples to turn from the individual "me" to the family "we."

Sorting out relational patterns, necessary for a healthy marriage, involves the question of identity. All humans strive, often unconsciously, to discover who they are and to find life's purpose. Some married couples form a deep bond between one another to assist this search, while others maintain separate lifestyles.

Without looking seriously at spousal identity, maintaining a stable marriage over a long period of time is difficult. Commitment to spouse and family is an essential prerequisite for the happy, lasting union of a man and woman. Remember that who you marry has a significant impact on who you are and who you will become.

Religious Identity

Questions about religion didn't concern me when I was young. I had already learned from my parents and *Baltimore Catechism* that I was a child of God, made in my creator's image. I believed the church's teachings and identified with my Catholic identity. I was a typical young Catholic of my generation. I didn't question who I was in my youth, for the world around me, especially my Catholic culture, gave me answers. I had no identity crisis.

Society, family and the church changed in the 1960s. Then, Catholics began asking who they were and what their place was in society and the church. At this time, traditional ways of doing things crumbled. The firm social and ecclesial norms, that directed Catholics through childhood, adolescence and adulthood, changed. As the world shifted focus, conflicting values challenged Catholics and their former stability ended. Easy divorce and birth control entered the scene. Catholics questioned church and civil authority. War, violence and fear threatened them. The mass media stressed a secular, relativistic lifestyle. With cultural myths and traditional rituals in disarray, Catholics searched for direction. The cultural changes, initiated in the 1960s, affected people's attitudes toward marriage.

On the positive side, today many couples recognize the need for greater maturity and more stability before they marry. If individuals do not know who they are, it is difficult to develop a mature relationship with another person in marriage. When two mature persons marry, it is easier for them to become one single unit in their love for one another.

When a man and woman marry, they establish a new relational identity, while remaining individuals. Their personal identity remains important, for it provides their uniqueness. After marriage, people remain who they are, regardless of their marriage relationship. Hence, it is unwise to believe that an abusive person will stop being abusive or that an alcoholic person will no longer drink after marriage. Temporary halts in such destructive activities during dating cannot guarantee that such behavior will not resume after marriage. Emotional and physical stress can flip people into their same old patterns.

Religion is a central aspect of who we are. Increasingly, however, couples enter marriage not sure of what they believe. Many lack a commitment to faith. In daily life, religion often takes a back seat. Marriage is the time to turn this around. Without seriously examining one's personal faith before marriage, a couple's family's religious identity may have little meaning afterwards. Failure to consider interfaith questions before marriage can bring dire consequences. Every couple needs to examine how their anticipated marriage will affect them and their children. Every situation differs and no simple answers exist. All mixed marriages involve religious issues that cannot be neglected. A man and woman's personal religious identity and the family relational identity are key factors when deciding whether to marry a particular person.

FOR REFLECTION

1. What is your personal story? What have you discovered about who you are?
2. How has your family story influenced your identity? Your partner's? How do you feel about becoming a member of your partner's family? How does your partner feel about joining yours?
3. How does your relationship with God influence your image of who you are? How is that a more stable foundation for identity than work, education, wealth or the opinion of others?
4. What thought have you given to the importance of raising a child with a strong religious identity? In what ways has your childhood experience of faith (or lack of faith) affected your life?

CREATING A FAITH-CENTERED HOME

A vibrant religious home environment introduces, nurtures and reinforces solid values. It offers a positive outlook on life, centered on faith. The marriage of two Catholics affords them the opportunity to develop such a home setting. So do mixed marriages, even though the challenges to doing so may be greater.

Difficulties exist in every family, even in the family of Jesus, Mary and Joseph. The Gospels of Matthew and Luke contain evidence of their difficulties. There were sinners and prostitutes in Jesus' lineage. The Incarnation took place before Mary and Joseph were married. At the Annunciation, the angel's greeting disturbed Mary. She knew that the child in her womb was conceived by the power of the Holy Spirit, and not by a man, but certainly it would not be easy to convince her family and friends of that.[42] When Joseph learned of Mary's pregnancy, he too was disturbed, but an angel reassured him that this child was of God.[43]

Jesus was born in an out-of-the-way place among strangers. His family fled for their lives to Egypt, then lived in Nazareth, a town not highly regarded at the time. Jesus upset his parents by staying behind in the Temple at the age of twelve (imagine misplacing a child for three days!) In so doing, he confused and distressed them.

Every family struggles in some way, as Jesus' did. None are perfect. The goal of family life is family health, not perfection, especially during difficult times. This takes a unique focus in interfaith families.

It has been said that there is no way to be a perfect family, but a million ways to be a good one. Creating a faith-centered home is an achievable goal, even for those coming from different faith traditions. In fact, given the importance of faith in developing identity, it is an indispensable goal.

The idea we have of ourselves is closely associated with the context, or environment, where we live and work. This we call "contextual identity." Those residing in the United States live, recreate, worship and work in a society free from oppression. Family, culture and world are the broadest context where we search for our identity.

The identity quest begins in the family. We grow as part of a family. We enter a new context, when we go to school. Each different situation helps us clarify our identity. We refine our sense of personal identity in the church we attend and the activities we pursue, whether these are sports, neighborhood projects or work responsibilities. We identify with school teams and work associates. In life's give and take, we find deep identity in ultimate and intimate relationships involving love, trust and forgiveness. We experience functional identity in our jobs. Identity contexts are limitless, even though some are more important than others. The family is at the top of the list. Here, we begin our search for identity.

Families vary greatly, depending on their location, socioeconomic condition, ethnic background and religious orientation. The basic orientation of a farm family differs from one living in a slum. A divorced or blended family has a different context than an intact, nuclear family. Within the same family, the context of parents and their children are not the same. The deepest relational patterns of spouses and children occur within the family. What happens here influences everything they do outside of the home. Here, family members develop personality traits, form attitudes, internalize religious rituals, learn basic beliefs and adjust to success and failure. How a family structures its relational context is vitally important to the value formation of the entire household. The family's home environment is the most significant context where human identity develops and growth occurs. Well-balanced families have a healthy family environment.

We engage in all of our activities within the context of space and time. This implies that we do not form personal or relational identity in a vacuum. It develops in real life situations within a definite time and place. Although family life differs from a hundred years ago, core beliefs remain unchanged, even though the way we live them out differs. Since identity is developmental, family identity must be considered within the context of modern life. This means remaining connected to core values, like honesty, kindness and justice, while living in today's world. We learn how to live a value-based life by following the dictates of our faith.

Contextual identity emerges largely by the internalization of preconscious environmental values, attitudes and ways of acting. This internalization process occurs in religious, political, social and economic situations. Although business, neighborhood, church, or family cultures vary greatly, each influences us through the attitudes and values that they convey. These environments tell us whether we are welcome or merely tolerated. Spatial configurations, decorations and personal reactions indicate more than words. Parental actions, sibling response and household settings indicate what values are important. Over time, such contextual influences affect our personal and relational identity.

Deep values and life orientation take shape through repeatable ritual actions. Regular family prayer, Sunday church attendance and blessings before meals impact children's attitudes and reinforce adult faith. Such repeatable actions are more important than what is taught in words. Hence, ritual patterns, not doctrine, set the foundation for our self-image. If a mother shows favoritism to a daughter over a son, this says more than telling the boy that he is a good person. Family ritual patterns and symbols are building blocks in establishing a healthy family environment.

We develop religious values and attitudes in response to such ritualistic activities. For couples professing different Christian faiths, their mutual prayer, a cross, Bible reading, sacred times like Good Friday, Easter and Christmas, and regular church attendance establish, maintain and develop a family's religious identity. As a child, no one told me to be proud that I was a Catholic, or told Jim, my friend down the street, to be proud that he was a Protestant. Our homes, religious practices and churches shouted this message to us, long before we knew what it meant.

I recall the importance of family rituals in our home, when I observe two statues depicting Jesus and Mary on our dining room mantle. Each is encased in a grotto about six inches high. They seem modern yet come from another era. Nothing similar is made today. The grottoes are made of turquoise stone, resembling the black clinkers that remain in a coal furnace after the ashes burn out. Someone meticulously assembled them and colored the old clinkers. The statues have been in their present location for two years. I found them when cleaning out the attic after Mom died. My parents carefully wrapped them in paper to protect them when we moved from our original home to our present one forty years ago. The statues were misplaced among the other moved items.

When I first saw them, I remembered that they once rested on our living room bookcase. I presumed that someone gave them to my Mom in her childhood. When my eighty-nine-year-old aunt saw them, she said, "Bob, these statues of Jesus and Mary sat in our home when I was a small child. I never remember a time that they were not on our hall table." The origin of the statues is unknown, but their significance is clear. Memory of them is imbedded in four generations of faithful Catholics. They symbolize something deeper than words.

That's what Catholic, Jewish, Protestant and other religious symbols and practices do for their members. Children and adults do not always understand the deep meaning of a symbol or ritual. This is secondary to the impact they have on telling a child what is important. They are part of a home environment, the bedrock of a family's religious identity.

The home's religious flavor applies to any faith context. Some parents do not pray or introduce their children into a formal religion. They often claim that they want to give their children the freedom to decide on a religious faith later on. In reality, their approach is not neutral, but speaks volumes to their children. It leaves children ignorant about basic beliefs and core values. When parents encourage children in other aspects of life, but avoid their religious formation, they send their children signals that religion is not important. Parents who do not provide faith formation for their children do them a disservice. Tricia, raised in such a household, learned in college that her friends took their faith seriously. When she experienced their knowledge and religious values, Tricia felt ignorant and hollow. She was very disappointed because of her parent's negligence, telling her best friend that they deprived her of an important aspect of childhood. She said, "I'll never make this mistake with my children."

Creating a religious home environment is a vital dimension of contextual identity. This is not present in many marriages today. Society's materialism, relativism and time pressures often substitute for a family's prayer life, religious images in the home, Bible study, teaching children about God and church attendance.

Developing a religious home environment is a special challenge for interfaith couples. They need to establish a household contextual identity that reinforces their personal religious identity and helps children sort through their religious values. In so doing, family members need to respect the different religious perspectives of the interfaith couple.

Before marriage, interfaith spouses need to decide upon their religious home environment. This includes how they plan to share the richness of their religious traditions with children. They can pray with their children, attend Sunday services, teach children values that are common to their differing faith traditions, indicate how their beliefs differ, decide on religious symbols for the home and help children avoid a relativistic attitude toward various faiths. Often, this never happens because parents are too busy, don't bother, do not take their responsibility seriously, don't know how or fail to ask themselves and their children the right questions.

Parental attitudes set the religious tone of a home. Parents are encouraged to buy religious books, pray and celebrate holy occasions with their children. They cannot abrogate this privilege to anyone else.

When searching among miscellaneous items at an auction, I noticed a packet containing ten white envelopes. The envelopes held about a hundred old holy cards of saints and prayers. Some were written in German. Others had paper lace decorations around their sides. There were saints for all occasions—good weather, various sicknesses and multiple blessings. I never heard of many of these saints. There were cards honoring Jesus, Mary, angels, Saint Anthony and others. Several cards contained the names of the priests and nuns that gave them to the recipient. No one else bid on the cards. I bought them.

Why did I buy them? I don't need devotional cards, I have plenty from my childhood. The cards, however, reminded me of a time past, where everything in my childhood was Catholic—our home, school, textbooks, teachers, friends and sporting activities. We hung around with Catholic kids, played in a Catholic schoolyard and rarely ventured up the street to play in the public school ground. For some reason, it seemed like a strange place to play, for it wasn't Catholic. Our external environment or contextual identity was almost totally Catholic. When we ventured beyond our Catholic comfort zone in thought or action, we were lost.

Over the years, I met many Jewish, Protestant, Muslim and Buddhist men and women who told me similar stories of their childhood and upbringing. In each case, religious ritual patterns shaped our actions and modes of thought. Our internal environment, as well as our personal and family identity, affected us. On a level deeper than rational, conscious thought, our religious traditions dictated our way of thinking, judging and acting.

Today, Catholics, Protestants and members of other faith traditions work and play side by side. The world is more fast-paced and complex. Whereas past generations often married within their own religious traditions, mixed marriages are becoming more common. It is now often difficult in such marriages to foster a family environment that helps people internalize religious, personal and family identity.

INTERNAL AND EXTERNAL HOME ENVIRONMENTS

Two dynamics that influence identity come into play in establishing a religious home environment. These are where and when we live. Human learning happens in a definite place and time, and these play a key role in our thought patterns, attitudes and actions.

We possess innate capabilities, which enable us to know things outside of ourselves. Just as our legs and feet enable us to walk, certain internal capabilities allow us take in sensory information from outside, process it and draw conclusions. Everything that we know is filtered through our experiences in space and time. Our human faculties cannot know anything without perceiving them in space and time configurations and cannot imagine anything outside of them. We acquire knowledge, develop attitudes and make decisions in space and time.

Family prayers, parental teaching about God, community worship, religious home practices, religious symbols and rituals, and church ministers influence us. They also affect how our parents, relatives and neighbors deal with their children and how we relate to our parents, brothers, sisters and friends.

We internalize our religious environment differently. Religious families develop an inner religious environment—a fundamental religious orientation that directs their attitude toward life itself. It influences their moral decisions, ways of acting on a date, proper business procedures, weekly church attendance and prayer. Our internal religious environment affects also our external home environment. In every family, children reflect similar values learned at home, even though they demonstrate them differently.

A vibrant religious family life creates a healthy environment that introduces, nurtures and reinforces solid values. These give birth to attitudes toward family members, neighbors, strangers, enemies and the larger community. Our churches and religious schools reinforce our values, first learned in the home.

The external environment refers to the place, space and time, where and when a family lives and works. The external environment can include the social conditions, neighborhood, living space, workplace, and the way that such space is arranged and decorated. It also includes how a neighborhood or individual home reflects a religious orientation through its churches, celebrations and other symbols of belief and practice. The external environment also includes the time spent in prayer, reflection, spiritual reading, meditation, preparation for religious celebrations, attendance at religious services and Bible study. This environment includes the ways that the space and time, where people live, work, and celebrate, manifest a religious orientation.[44]

In some Catholic, Protestant, Muslim, Jewish and interfaith families, the religious external environment is clear. Children and adults learn, work, pray and recreate in a well-determined environment. Family members know what it means to be a member of their respective faiths. In such families, faith is a way of life that extends from home to work, church and the broader society. In other families, the external home environment is not well ordered and the family's religious identity is not clearly established.

Internal environment refers to the conscious or unconscious attitudes or ways of acting that a person or a group internalizes, which influence their beliefs and practices. It includes a person's attitudes, orientation, and ways of thinking, deciding, and acting. This internal environment provides the fundamental orientation that a person or family takes toward many religious issues. This may include the priority given to Sunday church attendance, religious belief about life's sacredness, the importance of spending time at home in family activities and prayer, the need for adult faith formation, the value of a solid Catholic education, and regard for the pope, bishops, and clergy.[45]

Rapid social changes affect many families' external religious environment. When this happens, their internal religious environment may shift focus. Questions like, "What does it mean to be religious in a postmodern world?" and, "What is expected of people of faith?" surface.

In such a world, people may not know how to respond, and family prayer, church attendance and religious formation may become less important in their lives. When this happens, many question their religious identity, as their religious home environment weakens or almost disappears. Children raised in such homes often put little priority on faith, prayer or church attendance.

Today, the need to establish a healthy religious identity intensifies. To identify as religious persons with definite values and convictions means to know who we are, what we believe, what our faith teaches and what is our final destiny. Doing so is a lifelong task, one that begins early and solidifies throughout life.

CREATING A RELIGIOUS FAMILY ENVIRONMENT

No blueprint exists for creating a healthy interfaith home environment. It is possible, however, to identify certain perspectives that assist this task. In doing so, it is important to remember that family beliefs and practices shift focus over time, even though unchanging love and trust remain. The ever-flowing pace of culture challenges interfaith couples to incorporate the teachings and practices of their respective churches into family life. In this way they create a faith-filled home.

The following points suggest ways to create a faith-filled home environment:

Families of faith stress life's basic goodness in their attitudes, teaching and orientation. This helps establish a religious family identity. It encourages family members to see life's goodness as the foundation for their personal attitudes toward God, nature, humans and society. God is present in families from their inception. This wonderful belief in a loving God who loves all humans establishes the ground for their hope, which gives a positive orientation to families, thereby helping them develop a solid foundation for life.

Families of faith are faithful to their basic beliefs, teachings and practices of their faith. Their beliefs enable parents to establish family life on a loving foundation. Parents introduce children to such teachings and practices from their earliest years and help them know and internalize what it means to be persons of faith.

Families of faith develop a firm commitment to personal, spousal and family relationship with God through prayer, their beliefs, regular church attendance and good example. A healthy religious home environment provides the comfort level to allow for individual and family growth to happen. This climate enables family members to deal with conflict, pressures and differences. It requires the exercise of the virtues of trust and forgiveness. Here, family members develop healthy relationship with each other.

Such families establish a balance between their personal lives, family commitments and presence at church or church-related activities. Each spouse understands the beliefs and values of the other and appreciates how these values influence their attitudes and the entire family. In attempting to know where the other spouse is coming from, they communicate their personal and spiritual needs to their partners.

Families of faith enhance a religious home environment by arranging the family's living space to reflect a religious spirit. The presence of symbols, depicting the family's faith in God is central to such an environment.

Such families take seriously their home religious rituals and devotions of an ethnic kind. The latter help pass on a religious heritage from one generation to the next. In Christian interfaith families, the seasons of Advent, Christmas, Lent and Easter are significant.

Families of faith look to the parents to set the tone for family faith. The positive example of parents helps children appreciate their belief and practice. In families, it is not what parents say, but how they live, that affects children's attitudes. Parents accomplish little when they speak of social justice but show prejudice toward other ethnic or religious groups. They also recognize their problematic situation when one spouse practices one's faith and the other does not. This requires ongoing discussion between spouses to avoid conflict, to deal with children's questions about faith's importance and to maintain family religious home identity.

Families of faith make relationships with each other a higher priority than professional work. When both parents work outside the home, relational priority to family members insures that significant time is spent with one another.

Families of faith spend considerable time with each other in leisure, prayer, church activities, social functions and healthy interchange. They discuss what it means to be persons of faith and consider their responsibilities at school, play and work. The spouses value the worth of every person and make a firm commitment to their partner, as they strive toward holiness in their marriage and family.

Families of faith welcome family members, relatives and guests in their homes. This kind of welcome carries over into the family's dealings with those outside their home.

Families of faith engage in social works outside of the home. They concern themselves with the needs of the poor, elderly and missionary efforts.

Families of faith maintain a sense of humor in difficult times. The spouses set the tone for such an attitude that can maintain family peace, even when things do not go well.

Families of faith value marriage for its own sake. They hang together, despite their problems. Spouses, especially, value their marriage as a long-term commitment and not just a relationship, based largely on mutual affection that can be dissolved when the affection lags.

Families of faith (with two Christian parents) emphasize Scripture as the Word of God through reading the Bible and placing it in a prominent place in the home. They live by values that the Bible proclaims and mirror Jesus' home at Nazareth. Their actions reflect the values recognizable in the holy family. *Families of faith appreciate the beliefs of both parents.* In so doing, the spouses keep open the dialogue with the other person's faith and offer a positive example for their children, friends and neighbors. Such couples might invite the Catholic pastor and minister of the other spouse to dinner with the family. When moving into a new home, the couple can invite the pastor to bless the home and family.

Families of faith are clear on the faith that the children will practice. Parents ought to decide on this faith before children are born. Doing nothing, not discussing the issue seriously or failing to make a firm commitment on their children's faith tradition does a disservice to the children.

Families of faith balance their home environment with time they spend in church activities. Children develop an early impression of church from family members, especially parents. When this impression is positive, the children can more easily grow to have a healthy regard for the churches of both spouses and see family prayer as connected with parish worship celebrations.

Families of faith emphasize the priority of prayer in their homes. Parents and children pray together. They also focus their family's Sunday time on church and spiritual activities, not soccer or other sports activities. In so doing, such families make every effort to keep Sunday holy.

When Christian interfaith families strive to take seriously these points, they set the foundation for a healthy family environment. Here, they can internalize basic religious attitudes, beliefs and practices. In so doing, their home becomes a school of

Christian learning, where parents and children grow in Christian values, beliefs and moral principles.

There are other particular considerations, depending upon the couples' faith backgrounds. Couples will need to decide if religious symbols and practices will be found in their home. If a Catholic marries a Jew, will Catholic feasts be celebrated? What about Jewish feasts? How will they be celebrated? After marriage, how will the spouses practice their faith? Will they pray together? Will they attend each other's church?

A religious context for children's upbringing has to be established. This means that a Christian family develops a religious atmosphere, including prayer, scripture, learning about God, Jesus, Church, people's equality, love, forgiveness and right living. Symbols and rituals affirming a family's faith tradition set the foundation for children's religious identity.

The family bonding of a couple and their children includes the relationships between the couple, their children and their extended family. The climate where relationships occur is important. That's why a positive, supportive home is necessary. When family members support each other, their attitudes usually reflect a positive orientation. Early in marriage, one party learns whether the other spouse respects him or her. So do children. Such respect includes the attitude one partner exhibits toward his or her spouse's faith, family and ethnic background.

Interfaith couples begin this sorting out process by reflecting on their most important core values. These include trust, love, a positive spirit, support, forgiveness and more. After agreeing on spousal and family core values, they can look at their different faith traditions and affirm the common elements present there. Many core values, for example, are similar for Christians and Jews. Like values exist in Muslim, Buddhist and other religions. In this sorting process, spouses are encouraged to learn each other's religious beliefs and practices. Similar feasts and rituals occur in Christian churches, like Christmas, Epiphany and Easter. In every case, interfaith couples can adapt prayer forms that address their needs and basic beliefs.

Besides their relationship with each other, a couple's relational identity also includes the identity between themselves and their children. The relationship between a mother and her children differs from the children's relationship with their father. Parents cannot compete with each other for their children's affection or for their religious loyalties. Even though a father and mother relate differently to their children, their love for them must remain constant. Both parents need to reflect their core religious values to children and let them know that religion is important.

Bill, a nonbeliever, never professed any faith himself, but he supported his Catholic wife, Mary, as she took their children to Mass each Sunday. One day, Sean, their ten-year-old son, told Bill that he wasn't going to Mass anymore. When Bill asked why, Sean replied, "Dad, what are you doing today? Going fishing? If going to church on Sunday is not good enough for you, it's not good enough for me either. I want to be like you. Let's go fishing together."

Bill went to Mass that Sunday. Six months later, he became a Catholic. Later, he said, "When I realized what my negligence did to my son, I woke up. When I realized the value of religion, I could not wait to join the church and become a part of my family's faith life."

What would have happened if Sean had not told his dad he didn't want to go to Mass that Sunday? What if he was not so assertive? He may have continued to go, but with no real conviction of its importance, because the person he loved most in the world didn't consider it necessary. Subtle attitudes develop in children because of the nonreligious practice of their parents.

Personal faith develops as couples change and mature in various relationships of their lives. This give and take with family, neighbors, friends, work and society influences who each person becomes. This ever-flowing search for identity and purpose produces the unique persons that we are. Gordon W. Allport indicates the significant role that religion plays in this process. He indicates that as we search for meaning, we develop a certain philosophy of life.[46] One key philosophy is the religious one. It unifies life, for it includes everything good in its scope.

Each spouse must take seriously, respect and cherish the religion of the other party as the way that God touches that person. Each person's religious traditions are sacred. For this reason, Catholics should never pressure a partner of another faith tradition to convert just because of marriage. If a partner decides to become Catholic, it should be because the person feels called by God, not only to please the Catholic spouse.

The above words do not imply that the Catholic party, a friend or relative should not *invite* or even encourage the spouse to become Catholic. This came home to me years ago. Jake, a Catholic, attended Mass each Sunday with his non-Catholic wife, Elizabeth. Both were in their seventies. They also attended church social functions and other events. If it were not for the fact that Elizabeth never went to Communion, one would think she was Catholic.

After I got to know them, I regularly visited their home. On one occasion, I said to Elizabeth, "I've been impressed with your faith and dedication to our parish. Often, I wonder why you never became Catholic. You are most welcome in our church, whether you are a Catholic or not." She smiled and responded, "Father, I've been waiting forty-nine years for someone to invite me to join the church." In less than a year, Elizabeth became Catholic. Some people can be led to the Catholic church through an invitation or the good example of a Catholic. Elizabeth's husband gave her that good example, but never invited her to join the church.

The "Catholic Promises"

The promises that a Catholic party makes in a mixed marriage need to be addressed in a realistic way. Lois, a devout Catholic, dated Jim, a strong Protestant, for three years. When she brought up the children's religious education, Jim changed the subject. This concerned Lois, for his parents were staunch churchgoers, and his mother was domineering.

As Lois's love for Jim grew, the issue took a back seat, until they were engaged. Then, Jim sidestepped it. He told Lois that he wanted to marry in his church. She agreed on the condition that they would get the Catholic church's permission to do so. Jim went along with her. In their formal preparation, a Catholic husband-and-wife team helped them. When filling out the marriage papers, the promises a Catholic must make came up. Jim said nothing. Afterward, however, he told Lois, "I will never allow our kids to be baptized and raised as Catholics."

This troubled Lois. She was a sincere Catholic in love with Jim. She didn't want to call off the marriage. Unable to resolve the matter by herself, Lois sought advice from a Catholic priest. She asked him whether she could sign the promises in good faith. He told her that the 1983 *Code of Canon Law* rules for a Catholic marrying a Protestant do not require Lois to promise absolutely to have her children baptized and raised in the Catholic Church.

The *Code* requires that one spouse "declares that she is prepared to remove dangers of falling away from the faith and makes a sincere promise to do all in her power to have all the children baptized and brought up in the Catholic Church."[47] This shift from an absolute promise of the 1917 *Code* to "trying one's best" is significant.

At the same time, the *Code* no longer requires Jim, the Protestant party, to promise to raise the children of the marriage in the Catholic church, which was an earlier requirement. Instead, Jim is "to be informed at an appropriate time of these promises which the Catholic party has to make, so that it is clear that the other party is truly aware of the promise and obligation of the Catholic party."[48]

The question sometimes arises about a person of another faith, like Jim, who refuses to allow the children to be raised in the Catholic faith.[49] If this is the case, can the Catholic party, like Lois, marry him? Can she honestly sign the promises? If she does, knowing full well that Jim will not allow the children to be baptized and raised Catholic, is the marriage valid? The questions involve canonical and pastoral issues. They center around "whether a Catholic can, in good faith, promise to do all that he or she can to see to the Catholic baptism and formation of children, while realizing the likely futility of these efforts and whether his or her promise in these circumstances is sufficient basis for granting permission for the mixed marriage."

Responses from the Congregation of Divine Faith indicate that the phrase "to do all in his or her power" is to be understood literally. Permission for a mixed marriage can be granted even when it is foreseen that the Catholic's efforts to pass on the Catholic faith will probably be fruitless because of the commitment of the non-Catholic spouse to raise the children in his or her faith tradition.[50] Permission for such a wedding can be granted in such circumstances. Lois, the Catholic party, can sign the promises in good faith and marry Jim, if she chooses. The marriage is valid. After marriage, Lois doesn't have to act in such a way to fulfill her promises that she ruins her relationship with Jim and the family.

Beyond the marriage's legality, however, further questions arise. Is it *wise* for Lois to marry Jim? If such conflicts exist before marriage, what might happen afterward? Does Jim's attitude portend problems in other areas? Is it not prudent to reconsider the marriage?

The 1983 *Code* changed the responsibilities of both partners of a mixed marriage. These changes reflect the Vatican II *Decree on Ecumenism* and the document on religious freedom. These decrees respect the freedom of conscience of the party of another religious belief. We see evidence of such respect in the way today's church addresses mixed marriages.

When interfaith parents raise their children in the Catholic tradition, the Catholic party needs to instruct children in Catholic beliefs and practices from an early age. Such instruction includes prayer, home devotions and church attendance. While children practice their Catholic faith, they can learn also from the parent of the other faith tradition and occasionally attend his or her church. Commonly held spiritual values, rooted in the beliefs of religiously minded people, help mixed marriages succeed.

Some children are raised in another faith, in spite of the Catholic parent's effort to have the children baptized and raised as Catholics. In these cases, the Catholic parent must show children good example, affirm the core beliefs of both parent's religious traditions, make them aware of Catholic beliefs and practices and support the children in the faith they practice.

FURTHER SUGGESTIONS FOR A RELIGIOUS HOME ENVIRONMENT

Acknowledge the importance of mutual respect and love. Respecting family members is foundational in any relationship. Without respect, love becomes manipulation. Spousal respect leads a couple to acknowledge that God has blessed both partners. This realization enables them to see that they both worship the same God, need affirmation and strive for the same ultimate goal.

Interfaith couples need to strive to understand and respect the religious beliefs and practices of the other spouse. With such a foundation, love grows, even though a couple's religious orientation differs. Respect for each other flows into respect for family members and for people beyond the family. Children raised in such a home environment may follow the religious path of one parent, but they respect, love and admire both parents, because they find the image of God in them.

Develop mutual prayer patterns before marriage. This ought to begin while couples are dating. Regular prayer during dating roots their prayer life after marriage. Children, who see their parents praying, receive a special gift that cannot be measured in money. Some interfaith couples shy away from praying with the family because of religious differences. This need not happen, for common prayer is an effective way to keep a family together. It affirms that we are social and religious beings. Since the family is the church of the home, spouses and children need to pray as a family.

Focus on truth and honesty as family values. Religious families are committed to human dignity and worth. Whatever religious differences exist, truth and honesty are indispensable for a healthy family. Without them, any social group disintegrates. They are the bedrock of a family committed to loving each another and dedicated to the wider community.

Concur on the religious principles to be emphasized with the children, the faith they practice and the church they attend. Family unity is important, even when one spouse belongs to another faith tradition. Parents are encouraged to seriously consider what religious values in their respective faith traditions they intend to emphasize in their home. Agreeing on the religion of their children, and the way that both parents support their children's faith is important.

Commit the family to a style of living that gives high priority to prayer, life's deeper meaning and the purpose of human existence. Parents set the stage for this to happen. They do so by stepping back and acknowledging that more exists than the superficiality that surrounds them on the Internet, television, advertising and contemporary life. Reflection and prayer help busy people connect with God, who is the bond that holds families together. Prayer solidifies relationships, allows people to see life's priorities and helps them recognize the importance of God, who made and sustains them.

Take seriously the promise made by the Catholic party before marriage to be faithful to his or her faith and to do one's best to see to it that the children are instructed and raised as Catholics. This is a serious obligation, and no Catholic can take it lightly. While doing one's best to fulfill this responsibility, the Catholic spouse needs to remember that some other faith traditions place similar responsibilities on their members. When I taught in college, many young adults told me that they were baptized, but there was no religion practiced in their homes. This sometimes happened in interfaith families because their parents were not faithful to their faith. Some parents wander down the road of non-practice because they lack support or clash with the other spouse. Others have weak faith or are afraid of offending the other spouse. Hence, they neglect their faith and fail to provide religious instruction for their children.

Enhance the religious traditions of both spouses by developing interfaith religious practices in the home. Parents can agree upon common elements in both faith traditions. In this endeavor, they can compromise, when possible, and not water-down their beliefs and practices. Like any solid ecumenical endeavor, the goal is to take the best from both and enhance each faith tradition, not to minimize their religious beliefs.

Interfaith couples need to be true to their respective beliefs and values. Such fidelity leads children to respect both traditions.

At the same time, children formed clearly in one religious tradition, will know and be comfortable with the faith they profess. If they are raised Catholic in an interfaith household, a child must be able to say, "I am a Catholic." The same with a child raised in another faith tradition. Such clarity establishes a child's religious identity. In mixed marriages, regular church attendance is vital. When it stops, this sends a strong signal to children that shopping, secular activities, or Sunday morning sporting activities, are more important than a family's worship of God.

Maintain visible expressions in the home of the distinctive symbols of each spouse's religion. In so doing, spouses can develop a home environment and their family life around common core religious beliefs and practices. Such beliefs and practices are important. For Catholics, religious symbols remind the family of its heritage. These may include a crucifix, pictures, statues, Advent wreath, Christmas crib and Bible. Many Protestants use similar religious symbols and rituals. In particular, they revere the Bible, which can be placed in a prominent place in the home. In the Jewish faith, religious rituals and symbols abound. In the marriage between a Christian and Jew, Jewish symbols can remind the family of the close link between these faith traditions. Buddhism, Hinduism and Islam also use symbols, which can find a place in some homes.

Displaying religious symbols unique to the religions of interfaith couples, explaining them to family members, and using them in prayer and home rituals is a rich way to engage in ecumenical prayer. Such interfaith endeavors point to similar beliefs in both religious traditions. They also manifest the distinct ways that interfaith spouses pray, believe and practice religion.

Recognize the value of asking for God's assistance in daily life and in difficult times. Interfaith parents can develop family values that focus on daily prayer that asks for God's assistance everyday. This enables the family to love and trust God, who guides and supports them in good and bad times. Emphasizing daily prayer helps a family develop greater confidence in God and each other.

Reach out to others and be concerned for their temporal and eternal well-being. Jesus says, "Love thy neighbor as thyself," and, "Turn the other cheek." Other religions have similar beliefs that urge their followers to show concern for others, especially the downtrodden, sick and aged. Compassion leads to belief in human rights and justice. In a society, where injustice is common, justice must be inculcated into family life. Social justice flows out of belief in the dignity of every person, which Christianity and other religions profess. The Hebrew tradition teaches that human dignity rests in the fact that humans are created in God's image. Jesus laid the foundation for us to see that baptized persons have a special dignity as temples of the Holy Spirit and members of his Body, the church.

Parents in mixed marriages are responsible for the faith formation of their children, even if when they have to go it alone. This includes establishing a prayerful climate and a faith orientation in the home. It also means arranging for children's religious instructions and church attendance at age appropriate times. Such parents in mixed marriages need to incorporate the children into the church which the children attend.

Interfaith couples need to be faithful to their beliefs, grow in faith, provide good example, and actively take part in their church's liturgical, catechetical, service and social activities. By showing commitment to one's faith and introducing children to the faith they will practice, parents give confidence to their children. This helps them sort out their own beliefs as they mature. In mixed marriages, sorting out personal beliefs often is a problem for growing children. This is especially true when both parents are faithful to their faith and also committed to their children. It can also be problematic for children when they are raised in one faith tradition, but the spouse of the other faith is more committed to his or her faith. Both parents in an interfaith family have the responsibility to develop spiritual attitudes in their children. This challenge may intensify, as children grow older and begin to decide for themselves. It takes wise parents to help children grow into spiritually mature adults.

Parents in a mixed marriage need God's special help. This help, which moves them to develop a solid prayer life and roots loving home relationships, is the wellspring of wisdom and provides strength in good and trying times.

OVERCOMING FAITH OBSTACLES

Shauna and Brad were deeply in love. They dated for three years and respected and admired each other. Brad was Lutheran and Shauna was Catholic, but both had many doubts about their faith. Neither took their faith seriously, even though they occasionally went to church. Then, Brad's sister Jennifer was seriously injured in an automobile accident and Brad's faith changed.

For two months, he spent considerable time with his sister in the hospital. As a child, Brad had often prayed and gone to church with Jennifer. His commitment to her led him back to his Lutheran roots. At first, Shauna focused on how much she missed having more time to spend with Brad. She shied away from going to the hospital with him, and even found herself longing for the "old days" before Jennifer's tragedy. Gradually, Shauna's outlook changed. She recognized how deeply Brad was hurting and how great a comfort his faith was becoming. Her compassion for Brad and his sister made things easier for her. Each day became an opportunity to thank God and recognize beauty in the smallest event. She began to sit with Brad during his visits and pray that Jennifer would recover. In so doing, her Catholic faith increased.

Jennifer occasionally showed signs of coming out of her coma. One day, she opened her eyes, smiled gently and began to speak, sit up and walk. Through a miracle of God, science and medicine, Jennifer recovered.

Difficult experiences can be a testing ground for marriage. What happens in each partner's life before marriage remains important and can influence events years in the future. It is important for spouses to learn all they can about one another, so they can be a source of comfort during difficult times, rather than another source of concern.

BLENDED FAMILIES

A couple's spousal identity focuses on their relationship. For interfaith couples this is influenced by how they lived their previous lives. A married couple never builds a relationship in isolation. Their present environment, future aspirations, past experiences and family of origin affect their present relationship. When one or both have been married before, spouses approach marriage differently than if neither has been married. An interfaith couple's relational context is made more complicated, if one or both spouses have children by a prior marriage, especially when these children profess different faiths.

Often, interfaith couples who form a blended family do not think through faith issues associated with bringing their children into a new marital relationship. For them, addressing this issue is vital for a healthy marriage. A couple entering a second marriage has a serious obligation to care for the spiritual welfare of children from a previous marriage. If the new spouse does not recognize this, or demands that spousal love take precedence over a parent's love for one's children, serious issues often surface.

Entering a blended family need not involve an either/or choice of a spouse or children. The couple needs to strive toward a both/and perspective, considering the faith of children as important. In interfaith blended families, how children accept the new parent is a vital aspect of the family's health and happiness. The same applies to the way the new parent accepts the children and their different faith traditions. Spouses need to give priority to the faith of their blended family. This may involve discussion between spouses and children. When children enter a blended interfaith home, their parents can give them the gift of the love they share with each other. Spouses need to show such love to their children through words and actions. If they maintain their love, even when children compete for their affection or set one parent against the other, the children will be blessed. When children in blended interfaith families witness such love, they can recognize their blended family as a "we" and appreciate the common elements in the different faiths they profess.

Parents root their family's religious beliefs and practices by how they treat each other and their children. Children need to see their parents praying before meals, at bedtime, in sickness and on other occasions. Christian interfaith parents can encourage children to read religious books, put up shrines at Christmas and Easter, and prepare an Advent wreath. Religious rituals, instilled early in life, last a lifetime. I saw religious values in action when I worked as a youth in our family store. One occasion particularly impressed me.

I began helping in our family's dry goods store when I was in the eighth grade. Old Ben, the iceman (as I called him), sold ice in the summer and coal in the winter from his small two-wheeled cart. He'd pushed it up and down Poplar Street, near our store. I'd often hear him in the summer yelling "Ice, ice, cold ice." Ben sold chunks of ice to the people who still had iceboxes in their homes (usually those who could not afford refrigerators). They usually gave him fifteen cents for a chunk, but if they had no money, he would give the ice to them. Ben put the coins in the money pouch he hung on the handle of the cart. Often, children tagged along after Old Ben pleading, "Mr. Ben, it's real hot today, please give us some ice to eat." He'd always smile, take his ice pick, crack off a piece of ice and give a little to each child. They'd respond, "Thanks, Mr. Ben," and run off to play but, in ten minutes or so, they'd be back for more. Ben often gave away more ice than he sold.

Every year, right before Christmas, he'd bring a small pouch of coins into the store. He would pour the contents of his money pouch on the counter, and always said the same thing, "Mr. Hater, how much can I buy this year?" Every time, Dad looked at the change on the counter and, without counting, say, "Pick out what you need, and we'll see." Ben would go around the store collecting children's toys and clothes. When he finished, Dad's response was the always same. "Ben, you've got just the right amount of money. Merry Christmas!"

When Ben came into the store at Christmastime during my senior year of high school, his money pouch contained just a few dollars in coins; his stack of merchandise, however, was very large. After Ben purchased his Christmas gifts and left the store, I said, "Dad, that wasn't much money for all that merchandise. We lost money on the deal."

Dad smiled and answered, "Yes, Bob, I know, but Ben is a good man and has hardly any money. He puts his Christmas gifts to good use. You know who he is, don't you?"

"Sure, Dad," I replied, "He's Old Ben, the ice, coal and junk man."

I was surprised when Dad continued, "That's right, Bob, but Ben is much more."

Trying to justify myself, I continued, "He must have a big family, for he buys all those kids' clothes and toys."

Dad replied, "He isn't married, but he is a special man."

By now, I was exasperated trying to understand what Dad was telling me, so I remained silent. Dad continued, "Ben is the preacher in the little church down on Poplar Street. He dedicates his whole life to the poor of his small congregation. No more than twenty-five families are members. He gives the clothes and toys to the poor children in his church." Dad concluded, "I don't know if Ben can read or write very well. I know he can't count money. I do know, however, that Ben is a holy man. He has large sections of the Bible memorized. He inspires those who know him, because he not only preaches God's word in church, but he lives it every day of his life."

I never forgot Old Ben. He is a symbol of those who live Jesus' way in their lives. The story is important for me because of who Ben was, but even more because of who my father was. Our family did not have a lot of money and Dad used the money he made in the store for us. During each Christmas season when Dad had to make a profit, he gave a generous amount of merchandise to Ben. His actions taught us the value of generosity.

It is episodes like this that teach children who they are and what faith means to their family. The priorities that parents set are conveyed through their actions far more than words. A child raised in a home where religion is a source of conflict and bickering may not have much use for it in adulthood. One raised in a home where religious values permeate every decision usually will not stray far from the right path.

For Reflection

1. What experiences from your childhood helped you to understand your family's identity? How did that influence your own sense of self?

2. What are the differences between your family of origin and your partner's? How might these differences affect the home

you establish together? What family traditions do you want to maintain? Which ones are you willing to sacrifice?

3. How will your home reflect the faith of the family living there? In what way will the physical environment change? How will faith alter the way the family spends its time and resources?

4. What ideas for "blending" your two faith traditions appeal to you? Are there others you are willing to consider?

BEYOND THE HOME

From

a survey conducted among Greek Orthodox Catholic couples in mixed marriages, Charles J. Joanides, a Greek Orthodox priest, concluded that most interfaith couples "described a desire to remain attached to their religious tradition and ethnic backgrounds because these associations met certain personal needs that were important to their self-image and personal well-being."[51] He implies that their religious and ethnic heritage significantly influenced their identity. Participants in his survey were used to their customs and beliefs and were reluctant to change.

Naturally, couples must learn to adapt their expectations to one another and, to a certain extent, they can decide how faith will be handled in the home they establish. But, interfaith couples often are faced with concerns of extended family members. Many parents resist their children's mixed marriage, feeling that it threatens their family faith. When this happens, a couple must find a way to communicate with their parents while continuing to respect, honor and admire them.

Parental concerns must be faced squarely. Sometimes, good communication between the couple and their parents alleviates concerns that arise out of ignorance or the fear of their child's losing the faith. Many parents need reassurance that their child will maintain his or her faith. The couple can tell their parents that their home will contain spiritual beliefs and values which they learned from them and that their different faith traditions will enhance their personal beliefs. Interfaith couples need to consider their parents' experience, wisdom and suggestions, even if they do not follow them. Interfaith couples should not turn away from their families if difficulties arise. When interfaith couples marry, the spouses and their children become members of two extended families, both of which must be honored.

The issue of setting boundaries or limits on how much influence relatives exert in a couple's home may never come up. When, however, this issue of influence presents obstacles to a couple's faith or their children's faith formation, the couple may discuss the matter with the relatives involved and, if necessary, set limits on the time they see them. Healthy boundaries have to be established with extended family members who present difficulties. If not, one spouse may identify too strongly with the requests of his or her parents or relatives. Then, the other spouse may feel unsupported or not trusted. This can drive a wedge between the spouses and lead the offended party to question the trust of the other spouse in other matters. If boundaries are not set, one spouse may bend so far to satisfy extended family members that couple and family needs are compromised. Ultimately the decision as to the couple's faith and the faith formation of their children is the couple's and only the couple's.

WIDER FAITH COMMUNITY NEEDS

In mixed marriages, couples must address the challenges that membership in separate churches entails. Besides personal and relational issues, the fact that each spouse is active in a different church often adds other challenges. Nonetheless, spouses have to support each other's active church membership. Often, this is not easy. It's one thing to attend Sunday church services; it's another to participate actively in a church's life. What happens when one spouse is not comfortable in the other spouse's church? Is the matter swept under the rug or discussed? Issues like this are better addressed before marriage.

ETHNIC AND CULTURAL NEEDS

Cultural differences present added challenges to marriages when a Catholic marries a Jew, Muslim or Buddhist. The same applies to the marriage of a western American and an eastern European, African or Asian. Each culture brings its own needs and expectations. Many needs, values and lifestyle of these ethnic groups are not the same as the American way of life. In mixed marriages, where religious differences exist, such cultural challenges can be formidable.

The marriage of an American Catholic woman to an African man involves a different context than if the same woman married a Japanese man. The same applies to the marriage between a Catholic man and a reform Jewish woman. A specific context is involved in every marriage, for example, between a practicing Catholic and a strong fundamentalist Protestant. In addition, a couple's parents and family are important aspects of contextual identity. Each of these affects a marriage's direction.

FOR REFLECTION

1. Many Christian parents in mixed marriages do not offer adequate faith formation to their children. Do you tend to agree or disagree? Why?

2. Comment on the following. A couple has serious differences in how the other spouse is to practice one's faith or how faith is to be celebrated in their home, and are unable to resolve these differences adequately before marriage. Should they postpone or call off their marriage because of such unresolved religious differences?

3. How can interfaith families enhance the spiritual identity of their family, especially the Catholic dimension, in spite of the couple's differences in religious beliefs?

4. Do you think most Catholics take seriously and live up to the promises that they make to do their best to have their children baptized and raised as Catholics? Why or why not? Do parents of other faith traditions take this obligation more or less seriously?

Catholics

marrying someone of another faith is an increasingly prevalent phenomenon. Dealing with the very real issues this can present requires a clear understanding of church doctrine and practices, but also a gentle pastoral touch. Keeping a positive view of all marriages can help in smoothing the rough spots encountered in preparing couples for marriage.

Although it is desirable for a person to marry someone belonging to the same religious denomination (Catholic to Catholic or Lutheran to Lutheran), to regard mixed religion marriages negatively does them a disservice.[52] They are holy covenants and must be treated as such.

Marriages of Catholics and non-Catholics once took place in the parish rectory, not in the church. Gradually, they began taking place in church, but not at Mass. After Vatican II and into the 1980s many mixed marriages of Catholics and baptized Christians were celebrated at Mass, but the non-Catholic spouse did not receive Communion. After the 1983 *Code of Canon Law* was published, church policies recommended that no mixed marriages take place during Mass. This was done out of respect for the spouse of the other faith tradition, his or her family, and friends. The reception of Communion is a sign of unity with the ecclesial community. On a wedding day, the fact that one-half of the congregation does not belong to the Catholic community (and, hence, does not receive Communion) cannot be a sign of welcome or unity on a couple's wedding day. To celebrate a nuptial Mass, when only Catholics in attendance receive Communion, might be likened to inviting guests to a celebration and not allowing them to eat. To avoid such issues, generally speaking, mixed marriages do not take place at Mass.

In many dioceses, mixed marriages between Catholics and baptized Christians can be celebrated at Mass only with the permission of the bishop. In addition, only with his permission can a person, other than a Catholic, receive Communion in church during such a wedding. When mixed marriages are celebrated outside of Mass, deacons often officiate. While pastoral and practical reasons may exist for doing so, it is important to be sure couples do not conclude that their marriage is of lesser significance than the marriage of two Catholics.

Catholics involved in mixed marriages with baptized Christians need to consider the holy and sacramental nature of their union and regard them in a positive, graced way. If so, such marriages are seen in more open, loving way.

There are some challenges for pastoral ministers preparing couples for a mixed marriage and for the couples themselves. An important aspect of Christian marriages, namely, their covenantal and sacramental nature can cause confusion. Protestants, generally, use the word *covenant* to refer to marriage, but do not call it a sacrament. Catholics use both, but focus on marriage's sacramental nature. What happens when couples belonging to different Christian denominations take seriously the covenantal and sacramental nature of the marriage, but have different ideas as to how to live out their commitment?

Couples need solid catechesis prior to marriage and ongoing support afterwards. If couples from different Christian denominations know their particular religious traditions, they can better contribute to the faith of their family and the broader ecumenical movement. *The Apostolic Exhortation on the Family* reflects this when it says:

> Marriages between Catholics and other baptized persons have their particular nature, but they contain numerous elements that could well be made good use of and developed, both for their intrinsic value and for the contribution that they can make to the ecumenical movement. This is particularly true when both parties are faithful to their religious duties. Their common baptism and the dynamism of grace provide the spouses in these marriages with the basis and motivation for expressing their unity in the sphere of moral and spiritual values.[53]

A better appreciation of their spiritual unity in marriage begins with a Christian couple's realization of their oneness through their common baptism.[54] Hence, "...marriage is a powerful symbol of God's faithfulness, love and grace freely given and received. It is part of Christian discipleship as Christians live out their baptismal faith. The life of fidelity and forgiveness that marriage requires models the very essence of what it means to love as one in Christ."[55]

This does not minimize their challenges of mixed marriages between Catholics and baptized Christians, but roots them in the covenant bond of Christian love. This bond symbolizes Christ's love, who bestows on the couple the graces needed to be faithful to their marital calling.

Peggy and Joe, experienced Catholic marriage ministers, said that in preparing couples from different Christian traditions for marriage, the couples often recognize in some way that they—not the priest, deacon or minister—are the real ministers of marriage to each other. Usually they cannot put this clearly in words, but know it is the case. It is up to those preparing them for their marriage to clarify it for them.

As the *Apostolic Exhortation on the Family* states, "The sacrament of marriage is the specific source and original means of sanctification for Christian married couples and families..... The gift of Jesus Christ is not exhausted in the actual celebration of the sacrament of marriage, but rather accompanies the married couple throughout their lives."[56]

The consequences of Jesus' new covenant, won by his crucifixion, are inestimable for Christian marriages. God's creative and redemptive love is the source and foundation of the love between Christian spouses. Because Jesus loves them, couples from different Christian traditions can love each another in Christ. "Since it (Christian marriage) signifies and communicates grace, marriage between baptized persons is a true sacrament of the New Covenant."[57]

Christian marriages, viewed in light of God's love and the couple's covenant with Christ, afford hope, for, "By reason of their state in life and of their order, (Christian spouses) have their own special gifts in the People of God."[58] Christian couples receive the necessary helps from God to enable them to fulfill their vocation. This grace is ordered "to perfect the couple's love and strengthen their indissoluble unity."[59] Couples encourage each other on their mutual road to holiness. God's sacramental graces strengthen them to offer loving Christian witness to their spouse, children, family, neighbors, colleagues and friends.

God's grace moves couples of different Christian traditions toward unity, as it does in the ecumenical movement itself. Grace gives them strength to overcome differences, avoid sin and remain united in Christ's love. This grace won by Jesus' sacrifice deepens spousal love, as couples appreciate God's love, witnessed by Jesus' death on the cross. For Christian interfaith couples their home is a domestic church, where their family becomes a "...community of grace and prayer, a school of human virtues, and of Christian charity."[60]

The Catholic Rite of Marriage states:

> Married Christians, in virtue of the sacrament of matrimony, signify and share in the mystery of that unity and fruitful love which exists between Christ and his Church; they help each other to attain to holiness in their married life and in the rearing and education of their children; and they have their own special gift among the people of God.[61]

These words need not apply to the marriage of two Catholics alone. Positive insights for couples from different Christian traditions flow from the presider's address to the couple to be married. He says, "[Christ] has already consecrated you in baptism and now enriches and strengthens you by a special sacrament so that you may assume the duties of marriage in mutual and lasting fidelity...."[62]

WELCOME THE INTERFAITH COUPLE

Often, engaged couples do not know where to begin. The importance of a welcome and a pastoral attitude when couples approach a priest or deacon to marry them cannot be overstressed. A couple without a solid faith background should not be dismissed as people who do not take religion seriously. Many couples have underdeveloped faith and do not appreciate the blessings of a religious home environment simply because they have not experienced one. Their parents may not have practiced any faith at home. Many such couples are open to learn more about faith, for they sense a vacuum in their lives.

Even though a couple initially may request a church wedding because of status, custom or parental pressure, solid encouragement and preparation before marriage often helps them make a new faith commitment. Marriage can be the beginning of not only a couple's life together, but their also of their new life in Christ.

Welcome must be the bottom line attitude of every church when dealing with any engaged couple, but especially with interfaith couples. This begins with the secretary who takes the initial wedding information and extends to the priest or deacon who officiates at the ceremony. Genuine hospitality often dissipates negative attitudes of spouses of other faiths or their parents. When a priest or pastoral minister senses such an attitude, the simple gesture of offering to take the couple to lunch or dinner beforehand can break down major barriers that exist. I recall the importance of such a gesture, when one interfaith couple, years after their marriage, reminded me of the time that I took them to lunch before their initial marriage preparation meeting. They said that my action put their relationship with the church on a new, positive footing.

It is easy to fail to realize how vulnerable engaged couples are, particularly when they have not been active churchgoers. Even faithful churchgoers need reassurance that a parish is glad to have them and to share the joy of their wedding. With the shortage of priests and increased lay staff responsibilities, some pastoral ministers may become impatient or weary when large numbers of weddings come up. It may be difficult for a priest to remain enthusiastic when celebrating three or four Masses on a weekend (plus weddings and funerals). Nonetheless, a sense of routine cannot be conveyed to the couple. Regardless of the pastoral situation, every wedding is a special time in the couple's lives. Priests and pastoral ministers must extend welcome to those being married and encourage their staff and volunteers to do the same.

The *Guidelines for Interfaith Marriage* of the Diocese of Cleveland underlines the importance of welcome and hospitality in mixed marriages. "Interfaith marriages require that the couple, along with their respective families and friends, are all brought together in an atmosphere of charity and accommodation. The involvement of the respective ministers is essential to generate and maintain this atmosphere."[63]

From the beginning of marriage preparation to the wedding itself, hospitality is essential. It especially needs to extend to the spouse of the other faith, who ought to be invited to church activities and religious celebrations before and after marriage. An important time for hospitality, besides the couple's initial contact with the parish, is at the rehearsal and the dinner afterwards. Many parents of a spouse with a different faith belief, who are reluctant or prejudiced about their children marrying in a Catholic ceremony, change their attitude because of the welcome offered them at the rehearsal and wedding itself. If possible, the presider at the wedding should attend the rehearsal and the dinner afterwards, if invited. Informal time spent with parents and friends of other faith traditions builds relationships and dispels ambiguity. When this happens, the interfaith wedding ceremony can be a real communal celebration of love.

The significance of the rehearsal and dinner afterwards is stressed in the following words:

> Although wedding rehearsals are often tedious and exaggerated, they are important to the wedding party and the respective families. Often, a special dinner follows these rehearsals. The priest/deacon should take this opportunity to invite the minister or rabbi to attend the rehearsal. If the priest is invited to the dinner, he should remind the couple to extend the invitation to the minister or rabbi as well.[64]

The *Guidelines* then summarize the significance of welcome in the words,

> He [the priest or deacon] should express cordiality, sincere hospitality, and fellowship in Christ. The priest/deacon should be sensitive and gracious with the minister or rabbi,

the family, and other associated with the wedding party, realizing that they may feel uncomfortable in the unfamiliar setting of the Catholic liturgy and traditions."[65]

SOLID CATECHESIS

Father Mark reflected on the lack of faith and religious knowledge of many engaged couples. He said,

> It's hard to present the notions of covenant or sacramental marriages, if engaged couples don't understand basic Christian beliefs. Some regard the church service as the beginning of a big party, with minimal stress put on the spiritual aspects of the wedding celebration.

The spiritual preparation of couples before marriage has improved, but the church still has a long way to go. Solid catechetical endeavors, adult faith formation and effective homilies help couples see marriage in a spiritual light. Parishes need to approach mixed marriages in this way and take the necessary steps to support and spiritualize them. To this end, Catholic spouses married to partners of different Christian traditions contribute when they show leadership in assisting Catholic communities in acknowledging the need for such catechesis.

Engaged couples need strong spiritual preparation. This often includes more than filling out marital forms, holding several sessions with married couples and completing a FOCCUS inventory and a daylong pre-Cana session. Parish ministers may have to spend more time with an interfaith couple. Time in preparing a couple for their wedding may have to be flexible, taking into account each couple's unique needs. This includes sufficient opportunities to explore in some depth the challenges and opportunities that their mixed marriage will present them. A couple needs to see the positive aspects as well as the pitfalls and explore them with a seasoned marriage minister.

Marriage ministers who conduct such sessions need to be sensitive and open. They are to encourage the couple to learn about the basic religious beliefs and practices of both faith traditions, so as to respect and understand the other spouse's faith tradition. At the same time, they are to stress solid catechesis in the Catholic faith and encourage couples to attend a spiritual retreat. No matter how good parish preparation sessions are, parishes can constantly improve them. They must center on faith, basic belief, family life and the practical issues that interfaith couples will face. As Rebecca, a pastoral minister said, "It's vital that we take time with interfaith engaged couples. Since their faith traditions differ from ours, parish ministers must provide solid, complete instruction for them in order to help them better appreciate their individual, spousal and family faith."

Before Vatican II, a priest prepared couples for marriage. Each couple received about four instructions if both were Catholic. In mixed marriages, often six sessions were required. The two added sessions helped interfaith couples address challenges they faced and answered their questions. This added requirement showed special care for these couples. Today, most parishes require the same preparation for the marriage of interfaith couples and for two Catholics—even though the spiritual and psychological stresses on interfaith couples are more challenging. It is generally recommended that parishes spend more time with interfaith couples than with two Catholics planning to marry.

Regardless of a Christian couple's background, a covenantal and sacramental approach to marriage requires them to consider how they prepare for marriage. This consideration acknowledges that Catholic parishes may need to have two different approaches to preparing couples for sacramental marriages, namely, marriages between two Catholics and between a

Catholic and a baptized Christian. Each has a different orientation, although both are sacramental in the full sense.

Couples need a clear understanding of the challenges of their marriage.[66] They need to appreciate the covenantal and sacramental nature of their marriage. Marriage preparation can include a couple's retreat, day of recollection or pre-Cana sessions.

Parish leaders need to oversee those preparing such couples for marriage. Do they extend a special welcome to them? Do they understand their needs? Are these ministers adequately prepared? Do they have a positive or negative view of mixed religion marriages? How well do they nuance their teachings? Is their approach based on Christian hope? How do they instill a strong appreciation that valid marriages between baptized Christians are holy sacraments of God? How do they instruct couples to understand what it means to be a sacrament for each other and for their children?

INTERFAITH COUPLES

Couples coming from different Christian traditions bring spiritual strengths to their marriage. They are to be made aware of how their family backgrounds and previous experiences will influence their marriage and to recall past times when they knew God was with them, their families and friends. They are invited to remember the joy of birthdays and anniversaries, the happy times around religious celebrations, and vacations and relaxing days. Such good times often include time spent with parents, siblings, grandparents and other relatives. These intergenerational experiences help them grow spiritually. In reflecting on such times, they can appreciate better how God's loving presence roots their lives.

Spouses should respect their partners' religious beliefs and traditions. For this to happen, communication is essential. They need to develop their communication skills with each other and with God through prayer. A marriage's fruitfulness is generated from the couple's ability to respond to the living God that dwells at the core of every marriage. Growing together in prayer strengthens the bonds between couples. Praying is a powerful covenant bond, joining Christian couples in and to Christ. It reminds them that God has joined them in a holy life.

The family is a community engaged in dialogue with God.[67] This dialogue begins with God, continues through the spouses and children. The love, which results from this dialogue, is shared in the family and with other people. Rooting the family in love makes it easier for spouses and family members to spend time with each other, balance work, school and leisure, and reach out to relatives and those in need. As interfaith families continue to grow in their understanding of the different religious traditions that exist in their own household, they can better understand God's role in their home, and what God calls them to achieve. "One of the rewards that many Christian interfaith couples discover in their relationship is that they learn not only about their spouse's tradition but also more about their own."[68]

Engaged couples need to approach their marriage with a vision of what it takes to have a wonderful marriage. A vision is needed, for without one, life becomes aimless and boring. Couples need to dream for themselves about a family faith model to replace society's secular image of the family. In so doing, couples have to trust God, clarify their values and develop healthy life patterns. To change negative social values, loving spouses begin with themselves. Interfaith couples must be true to each other, as they live by the dictates of their respective faith traditions. This means respecting each other's religious beliefs, assuming responsibility for their children's faith, and sorting out their differing values. It's not easy to have a happy marriage, even when both parties practice the same faith. It's even more challenging when they do not.

PARENTAL CHALLENGES

A Muslim parent expressed his concern because his son was engaged to a Catholic woman. He said, "I respect his desire to marry a Catholic, but my problem is with the parents of his fiancée. I met them several times and they seem very closed to their daughter marrying my son. They won't discuss it with him, my wife or me. I wonder how things will go after marriage, when we celebrate different religious feasts and children come along. If little communication with her Catholic parents exists now, what will happen later?"

Parents of couples coming from different religious traditions are to be reminded of the holy and sacred nature of their children's upcoming marriage. If Christian parents see their children's marriage as rooted in Christ, they may more easily approve of and support the marriage.

Couples preparing for marriage are taking a serious step. They need to realize the importance of honest communication, family religious values, prayer and church attendance. They also must appreciate that when a couple marries, the man and woman also marry into one another's families. In mixed marriages, this means that each spouse marries into a different religious culture. The religious attitudes and background of each family are bound to influence the couple's own nuclear family unit. There will be birthdays and holidays to celebrate, financial issues to address, sickness and deaths of parents, siblings, and relatives to face. Some of these may cause conflict and stress with in-laws. Often, when couples can't be all things to their own family unit, their in-laws and extended family members as well, they have to make difficult decisions in favor of their own family unit. This may be especially true for interfaith families during religious holidays, like Christmas and Easter or Yom Kippur.

Religiously minded parents often give input into their grand-children's faith. This can be helpful as long as they do not exert undue pressure on their sons or daughters. A narrow line exists between giving good parental advice and putting too much pressure on adult children. Parents can offer advice on religious matters, but they need to let their adult children make the decisions. The couple needs to set boundaries for overzealous parents. Sincere interfaith couples often do quite well for themselves in working out their children's religion. It is important to decide how the children's religion will be handled before the couple marries. A priest or parish minister can facilitate these discussions with concerned parents.

COMMUNITY CHALLENGES

Pastoral ministers can introduce engaged couples to mentoring interfaith married couples living in the parish. Some parishes prepare teams of different mixed-marriage couples to assist engaged couples in similar faith circumstances to sort out the challenges of their upcoming interfaith marriage. Not only does this provide a valuable resource for the couple, but it also helps them to feel at home in the parish community, rather than outcasts with a "less than perfect" marriage.

To minister to newly married couples, many parishes have begun "New Marrieds" groups for Catholic and interfaith couples. If your parish has such a program, encourage the couples you counsel to attend. If you lack such a program, perhaps you could suggest that a group of married couples begin one under parish auspices. Some parishes sponsor an annual dinner for those married the previous year. As part of their overall plan for ministering to newly married couples, parishes often send a card to couples a few weeks after their wedding and to newly married Catholic and interfaith couples that now live within the parish boundaries.

SETTING GROUND RULES

Before marriage, both spouses need to be confident that their relationship fulfills the basic requirements necessary for a successful mixed marriage. These requirements include:

- respect for both religious traditions
- agreement on common faith elements
- reaffirmation of personal religious beliefs
- development of the family's religious atmosphere around shared religious beliefs
- appreciation for the religious practices of the other party
- agreement on the faith and religious education of their children
- discussion of the religious identity issue in the home
- incorporation of key elements of the faith perspectives of both parties into the home

A good counselor will encourage the couple to consider these issues. If they are not willing to do so, they need to ask whether they are ready to marry. When couples neglect these requirements, the trust necessary for a successful mixed marriage may be lacking. If the two cannot agree on such fundamentals, based as they are in spiritual values (and, therefore, more accommodating of the beliefs of others), the potential for disagreement on other issues looms large.

VENUE

Not infrequently, the date on which a couple wants to be married is not available because the church is booked. In this case, the pastoral minister can help the couple find an acceptable date, time, other parish, or even another priest or deacon, to officiate at the wedding ceremony.

When the wedding takes place in a parish outside the diocese where one or both spouses live, special procedures must be followed. In this case, the couple needs to contact the parish where the wedding is to take place and follow the parish's instructions for filling out necessary paperwork and taking marriage preparation classes. Advise couples to set a date and time with the parish prior to reserving a reception hall and place for the rehearsal dinner.

Explain to the couple their options. If the marriage takes place in the Catholic church, the priest presides and accepts the wedding vows. A Christian minister, or minister of another religion, is welcome to attend and participate, if the married couple so wishes. He or she can say prayers, greet the couple and do readings, but not receive the wedding vows. Sometimes, a Catholic priest of deacon is asked to preside at a mixed marriage outside in a wedding chapel, park, or garden. Generally speaking, the church does not permit Catholics to marry in such places without special permission of the bishop, which is rarely given.[69]

If the wedding takes place in another Christian church or other place, explain the proper procedures as well as the dispensations required. In all marriages involving a Catholic that take place outside a Catholic church, the minister of the other faith denomination presides at the wedding. The priest may (but need not) attend and participate, but may not preside at the couple's wedding vows. In mixed marriage between a Catholic and unbaptized person, a rabbi, civil magistrate or another approved minister presides and accepts the couple's vows, not the priest. Again, the priest may (but need not) attend and participate.

The final decision about a couple's readiness to marry in a Catholic ceremony rests with the local pastor and the presider. The latter are responsible to oversee the couple's spiritual preparation.

NECESSARY PAPERS

Early in a couple's preparation, the pastoral minister or another designated minister fills out the marriage papers. Some ministers give couples a sheet, containing pastoral, personal and canonical assessment items to be filled out by the couple, prior to the minister filling out the papers. After discussion with the couple, if it seems appropriate, contact the minister or rabbi of the non-Catholic party.

As part of the necessary paperwork, the Catholic party makes the promises required of him or her. The pastoral minister obtains the required dispensations and permissions. Both partners (if Christian) must provide their baptismal records. For the Catholic, this must be a recent copy of the baptismal record, dated within about the previous six months. If a Catholic or a person of another Christian faith tradition cannot produce a baptismal record, the testimony of two people will suffice.

In the initial session, clarify the liturgical norms and fees for the use of the church or organist. If the marriage takes place in a diocese other than where the couple lives, the paperwork and preparation often is done in a parish other than the one where the couple is married. If so, the finished paperwork is usually sent through the respective chanceries of the two dioceses.

IMMEDIATE PREPARATION FOR THE MARRIAGE

The pastoral minister handling the marriage preparation needs to be available to answer any questions that the engaged couple might have. This becomes more important as the wedding approaches. For this reason, a contact person often is designated for the couple during the first session. Inevitably, questions arise about the wedding's liturgical aspects, as well as specific issues like the placing of flowers or setting up a rehearsal. Many couples ask questions about what music can and cannot be used at their wedding. Diocesan and parish norms vary on this issue. The couple needs to be able to contact the priest or deacon who is to preside at the ceremony. The presider, if he does not handle the couple's preparation, has to be made aware of their history, so that he can address them more personally at the wedding ceremony.

On rehearsal day, encourage the couple and the wedding party to arrive fifteen minutes before the practice begins. Inevitably, someone is late, so this time frame helps avoid rushing through practice to get to the rehearsal dinner on time. The presider for the ceremony is encouraged to attend or conduct the rehearsal. Many parishes have a wedding coordinator who plans and conducts the rehearsal, in which case, the presider can at least stop in and welcome those attending the practice. For many people of other faiths attending a rehearsal practice, the welcoming attitude of the rehearsal practice carries over to the wedding ceremony. For the family, hospitality begins here, not at the wedding.

Wedding rehearsals vary from parish to parish. Some parishes have suggested ways for entering the church, walking down the aisle, and other aspects of the celebration. Other parishes do not. Couples need to be apprised of various options during their marriage preparation. Whether or not the rehearsal includes practicing the readings, petitions and such varies from parish to parish. Before the rehearsal, the procedures that the couple prefers and what the parish allows need to be agreed upon with priest, the pastoral minister, or person handling the rehearsal.

WEDDING LITURGY

The *Rite for Marriage* distinguishes between the marriage of a Catholic to a baptized and to a nonbaptized person. Each is considered separately.

Marriage of a Catholic and Baptized Person

As discussed above in this book, any mixed marriage generally does not take place within Mass. The issue of receiving Communion at a wedding Mass can present difficulties. Among other reasons, the church, ordinarily, does not permit

Communion to be given to members of other Christian denominations not in union with Rome. With permission, a wedding may be celebrated within Mass, but only the Catholics in attendance are permitted to receive Communion.

The Rite for Marriage stresses the sacramental nature of marriage. Referring to the wedding liturgy itself, it says, "The liturgy of the word is extremely helpful in emphasizing the meaning of the sacrament and the obligations of marriage."

If the marriage is celebrated during Mass, the regular nuptial Mass norms are used. The priest wears white vestments. As already indicated, most marriages between a Catholic and a baptized non-Catholic take place without celebrating a Mass. In this case, the priest or deacon greets the couple at the rear of church or near the altar. The celebration begins with the liturgy of the Word. It may include three Scripture readings, one being the Gospel. After the Gospel, the priest or deacon gives a homily stressing the holy and sacramental nature of marriage and the privileges and responsibilities of the spouses. The ceremony continues with the priest accepting the consent of the wedding couple, the blessing and exchange of wedding rings, the general intercessions and a nuptial blessing. The celebration concludes with the Lord's Prayer and final blessing.[70]

Marriage of a Catholic and Unbaptized Person
This category includes the marriage between a Catholic and an unbaptized person (either a catechumen or a non-Christian). Such weddings use appropriate language and rituals to fit the specific context of the ceremony. The way the wedding is celebrated takes into account the sensitivities of non-Christians who may not believe in Jesus. These weddings follow the same general format as the marriage of a Catholic and a baptized Christian. This includes a rite of welcome, liturgy of the Word, receiving the

couple's consent, blessing and exchange of rings, and conclusion of the ceremony.

AFTER THE CEREMONY

Just as the couple should not view the wedding ceremony as an end to their courtship, but rather as the beginning of their life together, so should parish ministers continue their relationship with the couple. Often, even when the bride and groom are Catholic, the pastor sees them leave the church after the wedding and does not see them again until they bring a child for baptism. Make sure that you continue to invite the couple to active participation in the parish. If they do not respond immediately, it is still wise to make contact periodically. A parish might make a point of sending cards to its couples on the occasion of their wedding anniversary, or send reminders of upcoming couples' events or retreats. Make sure that both parties feel comfortable returning to the church for counseling in the event of marital difficulties.

In marrying, these couples not only join their families to one another, but they join them to the parish family. An abiding Christian hospitality will serve the couple well and reflect positively on the church.

FOR REFLECTION

1. One parish offers this suggestion: Compile a list of all non-members of your church that are married to members of your church. Invite them to attend certain religious celebrations during the year. Welcome them, also, at special social and other church events. If appropriate, ask them to help out at some church functions, especially those that involve their spouse or children. If appropriate, devise ways to ask them to help members of your church to understand any differences between their faith practices and those of your church.

2. Does your parish offer retreats for couples of different Christian traditions? Are there programs in place to support Catholic couples that could be adapted to serve interfaith couples?

3. To what degree does your parish marriage preparation for couples of different Christian traditions include hints on how to establish a faith-filled home environment? If these are lacking in the parish approach, how can they be included?

4. Can your parish leadership team offer a mentoring program for newly married couples? Perhaps you could invite several interfaith couples who have successfully worked out their religious identity to meet with engaged or newly married couples.

5. When children of interfaith couples are preparing to receive one of the sacraments, do you make sure their non-Catholic parents are made to feel welcome? Are these parents invited to learn more about Catholic belief and why the sacrament is administered? If not, is this a possibility in your parish?

What

better way to conclude a book on marriages than to remember Jesus' holy family at Nazareth? There, amidst joys and troubles, he prepared for his mission. In our homes, too, we prepare for ours.

Pope Paul VI says,

Nazareth is a kind of school where we may begin to discover what Christ's life was like and even to understand his Gospel. Here we can observe and ponder the simple appeal of the way God's son came to be known, profound yet full of hidden meaning. And gradually we may even learn to imitate him.

Here we can learn to realize who Christ really is. And here we can sense and take account of the conditions and circumstances that surrounded and affected his life on earth: the places, the tenor of the times, the culture, the language, religious customs, in brief everything which Jesus used to make himself known to the world. Here everything speaks to us, everything has meaning. Here we can learn the importance of spiritual discipline for all who wish to follow Christ and to live by the teachings of the Gospel.

...But I cannot leave without recalling, briefly, and in passing, some thoughts I take with me from Nazareth.

First, we learn from its silence. If only we could once again appreciate its great value. We need this wonderful state of mind, beset as we are by the cacophony of strident protests and conflicting claims so characteristic of these turbulent times. The silence of Nazareth should teach us how to meditate in peace and quiet, to reflect on the deeply spiritual, to be open to the voice of God's inner wisdom and the counsel of his true teachers. Nazareth can teach us the value of study and preparation, of meditation, of a well-ordered personal spiritual life, and of silent prayer that is known only to God.

Second, we learn about family life. May Nazareth serve as a model of what the family should be. May it show us the family's holy and enduring character and exemplifying its basic function in society: a community of love and sharing, beautiful for the problems it poses and the rewards it brings; in sum, the perfect setting for rearing children—for there is no substitute.

Finally, in Nazareth, the home of the craftsman's son, we learn about work and the discipline it entails. I would especially like to recognize its value—demanding yet redeeming—and to give it proper respect. I would like to remind everyone that work has its own dignity. On the other hand, it is not an end in itself. Its value and free character, however, derive not only from its place in the economic system, as they say, but rather from the purpose it serves."[71]

May the Father, Son and Holy Spirit bless all families and make them holy! May the families that this book touches reflect the family of Nazareth and bring peace, love and happiness to a society in need of hope!

[B I B L I O G R A P H Y]

This list includes a wealth of resources for interfaith couples and those who minister to them. Because of the diversity of opinions and faiths represented, some material may contain views not in agreement with Catholic faith or teaching. Couples should always rely on the advice of their marriage preparation counselor and priest.

For Couples

Allport, Gordon Willard. *The Individual and His Religion: A Psychological Interpretation* (New York: Macmillan, 1967).

Bendroth, Margaret. *Faith Traditions and the Family* (Louisville: Westminster John Knox, 1996).

Bush, John C. and Patrick R. Cooney, eds. *Interchurch Families: Resources for Ecumenical Hope: Catholic/Reformed Dialogue in the United States* (Louisville: Westminster John Knox, 2002).

Champlin, Joseph M., *Together for Life* (Notre Dame, Ind.: Ave Maria, 1997).

A Christian Declaration on Marriage, Origins, Nov. 23, 2000, Vol. 20: No. 24, p. 338.

Cowan, Paul and Rachel. *Mixed Blessings: Overcoming the Stumbling Blocks in an Interfaith Marriage* (New York: Penguin, 1989).

Crohn, Joel, Ph.D. *Mixed Matches: How to Create Successful Interracial, Interethnic, and Interfaith Relationships* (New York: Ballantine, 1995).

Family Life Office, FOCCUS (Facilitating Open Couple Communication, Understanding and Study), Omaha, Nebraska, 1985, 2 Ed, 1997.

Ford, John T. and Darlis J. Swan, eds. *Twelve Tales Untold: A Study Guide for Ecumenical Reception* (Grand Rapids: Eerdmans, 1993).

Glaser, Gabrielle. *Strangers to the Tribe: Portraits of Interfaith Marriage* (Boston: Houghton Mifflin, 1997).

Hater, Robert J., Ph.D. *The Catholic Family in a Changing World* (New York: Harcourt, 2005).

Hawxhurst, Joan C. *The Interfaith Family Guidebook: Practical Advice for Jewish and Christian Partners* (Kalamazoo, Mich.: Dovetail, 1998).

Joanides, Charles. *When You Intermarry: A Resource for Inter-Christian, Intercultural Couples, Parents and Families* (New York: Greek Orthodox Archdiocese of America, 2002).

Kilcourse, George. *Double Belonging: Interchurch Families and Christian Unity* (Mahwah, N.J.: Paulist, 1992).

King, Andrea. *If I'm Jewish and You're Christian, What Are the Kids?: A Parenting Guide for Interfaith Families* (New York: Urj Press, 1993).

Kippley, John F. *Marriage Is for Keeps: Foundations for Christian Marriage* (Cincinnati: Foundation for the Family, 1993).

Law, Maureen and Lanny., *God Knows Your Marriage Isn't Always Easy* (Notre Dame, Ind.: Sorin, 2002).

Lawler, Michael. *Marriage and the Catholic Church: Disputed Questions* (Collegeville, Minn.: Liturgical Press, 2002).

Lerner, Devon A. *Celebrating Interfaith Marriages: Creating Your Jewish/Christian Ceremony* (New York: Owl, 1999).

Levin, Sunie. *Mingled Roots: A Guide for Grandparents of Interfaith Grandchildren* (New York: Urj Press, 2003).

Macomb, Rev. Susanna. *Joining Hands and Hearts: Interfaith, Intercultural Wedding Celebrations: A Practical Guide for Couples* (New York: Simon and Schuster, 2003).

McClain, Ellen Jaffe. *Embracing the Stranger: Intermarriage and the Future of the American Jewish Community* (New York: Basic, 1995).

Petsonk, Judy and Jim Remsen. *The Intermarriage Handbook: A Guide for Jews and Christians* (New York: Harper, 1991).

Popcak, Gregory K. *For Better...Forever!: A Catholic Guide to Lifelong Marriage* (Huntington, Ind.: Our Sunday Visitor, 1999).

Reuben, Steven Carr. *Making Interfaith Marriage Work: A Nonjudgmental Guide to Coping with the Spiritual, Emotional, and Psychological Issues* (New York: Prima, 1994).

Richardson, Brenda Lane. *Guess Who's Coming to Dinner: Celebrating Interethnic, Interfaith, and Interracial Relationships* (Berkeley, Calif.: Wildcat Canyon Press, 2000).

Roberts, Cokie and Steve. *From this Day Forward* (New York: Harper Perennial, 2000).

Rozakis, Laurie E. *Complete Idiot's Guide to Interfaith Relationships* (New York: Alpha, 2001).

Salkin, Rabbi Jeffrey K. *Putting God on the Guest List* (Woodstock, Vt.: Jewish Lights, 1993).

Strobel, Lee and Leslie. *Surviving a Spiritual Mismatch in Marriage* (Grand Rapids: Zondervan, 2002).

The Catholic Couples Bible (Wichita, Kan.: Fireside Catholic Publishing, 2003).

Vondenberger, Victoria, R.S.M., J.C.L. *Catholics, Marriage and Divorce: Real People, Real Questions* (Cincinnati: St. Anthony Messenger Press, 2003).

Weiss, Vikki and Jennifer A. Block. *What to Do When You're Dating a Jew: Everything You Need to Know from Matzah Balls to Marriage* (New York: Three Rivers, 2000).

Witte, John, Jr., et al., eds., *Covenant Marriage in Comparative Perspective* (Grand Rapids, Mich.: Eerdmans, 2005).

For Parish Ministers
Bush, John C. and Patrick R. Cooney, eds. *Interchurch Families: Resources for Ecumenical Hope: Catholic/Reformed Dialogue in the United States* (Louisville: Westminster John Knox, 2002).

Joanides, Charles. *Ministering to Intermarried Couples: A Resource for Clergy and Lay Workers* (Brookline, Mass.: Holy Cross Orthodox Press, 2003).

Wicker, Les C. *Preparing Couples for Marriage: A Guide for Pastors for Premarital Counseling* (Lima, Ohio: CSS Publishing, 2003).

1. Taken from Archdiocese of Cincinnati statistical records. Today, many people think little of dating or marrying someone outside of their faith tradition. The above statistical data indicates this trend. While this was happening, the number of Catholic and mixed marriages fell from 2,969 in 2000 to 2,592 in 2003.

2. An approach that treats interfaith couples like second-class citizens or fails to welcome them can lead the couple to search elsewhere in their journey of faith.

3. *Pastoral Constitution on the Church in the Modern World* (*Gaudium et Spes*), 48. From Austin Flannery, ed., *Vatican Council II: The Conciliar and Post Concilair Documents* (Northport, N.Y.: Costello, 1988).

4. 1983 *Code of Canon Law,* Chapter VI, 1124–1129, and Canon 1086.

5. Canons 1124–1129 and 1086.

6. The glossary of the *Catechism of the Catholic Church* (CCC) describes apostolic succession as "The handing on of apostolic preaching and authority from the Apostles to their successors the bishops through the laying on of hands, as a permanent office in the Church." *Catechism of the Catholic Church,* second edition (Washington, D.C.: USCCB, 2000), p. 867.

7. CCC, 123, p. 152.

8. *Guidelines for Interfaith Marriage*, 14. (Cleveland: Diocese of Cleveland, 1997).

9. *Guidelines for Interfaith Marriage*, 16.

10. The expressions "interfaith couple" and "interfaith family" are not included explicitly in the *Code*. As used in this book, however, these terms are consistent with what is in the *Code*, even though not literally found there. The 1983 *Code of Canon Law* is cited throughout this book. The entire text of the code is available online at http://www.vatican.va/ archive/ENG1104/_INDEX.HTM. Canon 1124 refers to marriages "between two baptized persons, one of whom was baptized in the Catholic Church or received into it after baptism and has not left it by a formal act, and the other of whom is member of a church or ecclesial community which is not in full communion with the Catholic Church" (Canon 1124, 1983 *Code of Canon Law*).

11. *Gaudium et Spes* explores the beauty of Christian marriage. It says, "Christ our Lord abundantly blesses this love (between spouses), which is rich in its various features, coming as it does from the spring of divine love and modeled on Christ's own union with the Church. Just as of old God encountered his people with a covenant of love and fidelity, so our Savior, the spouse of the Church, now encounters Christian spouses through the sacrament of marriage. He abides with them in order that by their mutual self-giving spouses will love each other with enduring fidelity, as he loved the Church and delivered himself for it. Authentic married love is caught up into divine love and directed and enriched by the redemptive power of Christ and the salvific action of the Church, with the result that the spouses are effectively led to God and are helped and strengthened in their lofty role as fathers and mothers" (*Gaudium et Spes*, 48).

12. *Guidelines for Interfaith Marriage*, 17.

13. For more complete treatment of the specific situations in marriages of Catholics to members of various faith traditions, see *Marriage Preparation Guidelines: Throughout the Lifecycle*, Archdiocese of Cincinnati, Appendix D, Ecumenical and Interfaith Guidelines, pp. 82 ff. These diocesan guidelines treat the pastoral, liturgical and canonical considerations to be addressed in each specific category of marriage (for example, the marriage of a Catholic to an unbaptized person of no religion, to an atheist or agnostic, to a catechumen, to an eastern Catholic, to a baptized Protestant, and so on).

14. John C. Bush, and Patrick R. Cooney, eds. *Interchurch Families: Resources for Ecumenical Hope: Catholic/ Reformed Dialogue in the United States* (Louisville: Westminster John Knox Press, 2002), p. 1.

15. Bush, p. 51.

16. Bush, p. 51.

17. *Marriage Preparation Guidelines* says, "The Catholic Church does not encourage ecumenical or mixed marriages. For such a marriage to be valid, a permission or dispensation has to be obtained for such a marriage" (see canons 1086, 1124 and 1125), p. 86.

18. "The intimate community of life and love which constitutes the married state has been established by the Creator and endowed by him with its own proper laws.... God himself is the author of marriage" (*Gaudium et Spes*, 48).

19. *CCC*, 1604.

20. As a sign of God's love, Yahweh established the covenant of the Old Law, symbolized by the "image of exclusive and faithful married love..." (*CCC*, 161).

21. *Humanae Vitae*, 8.

22. *Humanae Vitae*, 9.

23. Joan C. Hawxhurst, *The Interfaith Family Guidebook Practical Advice for Jewish and Christian Partners* (Kalamazoo, Mich.: Dovetail, 1998).

24. See entire text at www.interchurchfamilies.org/journal/ 2004jan02.shtm.

25. www.interchurchfamilies.org/journal/2004jan02.shtm.

26. *Apostolic Exhortation on the Family*, n. 78.

27. *Catholic Evangelization in an Ecumenical and Interreligious Society* (Washington, D.C.: USCCB, 2004). This document offers positive suggestions for sharing Jesus' Good News within a pluralistic world. It has applications for mixed marriages.

28. "Sacraments are efficacious signs of grace, instituted by Christ and entrusted to the Church, by which divine life is dispensed to us" (*CCC*, 1131). Sacraments give us God's own life and help us do good and avoid evil. There are seven sacraments. They employ visible signs, like water and bread.

29. Bush, p. 50.

30. Ephesians 5:25–32.

31. Pius XI, *On Christian Marriage*, 13.

32. *On Christian Marriage*, 13.

33. Paul VI, *Humanae Vitae*, 25.

34. *CCC*, 1534.

35. *Gaudium et Spes*, 48. In addition to the Flannery edition, all documents of Vatican II are available at www.vatican.va.

36. Matthew 28:19–20.

37. Judy Petsonk and Jim Remsen, *The Intermarriage Handbook: A Guide for Jews and Christians* (New York: Harper, 1991) p. 192.

38. Petsonk, p. 192.

39. Petsonk, p. 194.

40. Petsonk, p. 194.

41. Petsonk, p. 194.

42. Luke 1:28 ff.

43. Matthew 1:18 ff.

44. Robert J. Hater, *The Catholic Family in a Changing World* (New York: Harcourt, 2005), p. 113.

45. Hater, p. 114.

46. Gordon W. Allport, *The Individual and His Religion: A Psychological Interpretation* (New York: MacMillan, 1967).

47. Canon 1125, #1.

48. Canon 1125, #2.

49. John P. Beal, et al., eds. *New Commentary of the Code of Canon Law* (Mahwah, N.J.: Paulist, 2000), p. 1346.

50. Beal, p. 1347, et seq.

51. Beal, p. 67.

52. While not encouraging mixed marriages, great care must be taken not to paint them in a negative light when the interfaith couple comes to be married. *Marriage Preparation Guidelines* says, "The Catholic Church does not encourage ecumenical or mixed marriages. For such a marriage to be valid, a permission or dispensation has to be obtained for such a marriage. (See canons 1086,1124 and 1125), p. 86.

53. *Origins*, December 24, 1981 (Volume 11: 28 & 29, # 78).

54. To reiterate this point, *Marriage Preparation Guidelines* says, "Remote marriage preparation begins in early childhood and includes all those family as well as environmental factors that influence and prepare the person in positive and negative ways for marriage."

55. Bush, p. 53.

56. John Paul II, *Apostolic Exhortation on the Family,* 56.

57. CCC, 1617.

58. *Lumen Gentium*, 11.

59. *CCC*, 1641.

60. *CCC*, 1666.

61. From Catholic Rite of Marriage in *Rites of the Catholic Church*, volume one (Collegeville, Minn.: Liturgical Press, 1990), 1.

62. Catholic Rite of Marriage, 43.

63. Catholic Rite of Marriage, 64.

64. *Guidelines for Interfaith Marriage*, 73.

65. *Guidelines for Interfaith Marriage*, 75.

66. Because of the many challenges that surface in mixed-religion marriages, parishes might consider adding additional meetings or sessions for preparing interfaith couples, and offering follow-up sessions after marriage. What is said above about preparing Christian interfaith couples is valuable for all couples preparing for marriage, especially lapsed or lax Catholics.

67. Cf. John Paul II, *Apostolic Exhortation on the Family.*

68. Bush, p. 3.

69. For further explanation, see *Marriage Preparation Guidelines*, pp. 87, et seq.

70. Catholic Rite of Marriage, 8, 11, 39, 41–42, 51–54.

71. Spoken in an address on Nazareth, January 5, 1964. The Liturgy of the Hours contains this address, read each year on the Feast of the Holy Family, the Sunday after Christmas.